Table of contents

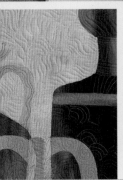

Dedication

To my husband Brian, who for 25 years has been generous, loving, tolerant, supportive, and has made room in his life for all my stuff, and works hard so I don't have to. He's a mensch.

To my children, Joshua and Samantha, who have always treated my work with respect and have made me very proud.

To Mary McManus, who has helped me from the very start, sharing ideas, tools, fabric, encouragement, and going to quilt shows.

Acknowledgments

I feel very privileged to have had the chance to write this book. Left to my own devices it would still be an idea floating around in my head.

Making quilts, learning and developing techniques, and then sharing them with others through my writing, teaching, and lecturing has given me great joy. What a wonderful thing to find something you love to do and be given the opportunity to spend time doing it. I consider myself lucky to be a member of the community of quilters.

Patricia and John Bolton, publishers of this book, have let me write on a regular basis for QUILTING ARTS MAGAZINE®, have published my "Groovy Guitars" pattern, and have even bought my quilts. They have always treated me fairly, kindly, patiently, and with a sense of humor. I thank them, and wish them continued success. I hope they'll be proud of this book, too.

Jennifer Bixby is an excellent editor. She knows what I really meant to say, knows what to keep and what to throw out. She makes my writing funnier and wittier, and has made this process a lot of fun. Thank you for wading through all the static to find the clear signal.

I am thrilled with what designer Larissa Davis has done for this book. She is a fabulous designer, and is truly talented. Thanks so much for doing such a great job.

Judy Koser, Pat Valerio, and the other Tuesday Night Quilters have provided friendship and advice, got me started, and pushed me to keep going. Without them I'd be an engineer in an office somewhere, wearing an itchy suit.

Karey Bresenhan has opened a lot of doors for me that I have enjoyed walking through. I can't thank you enough.

I believe you are very lucky if you have one friend in the world who knows everything about you and still puts up with you. Lynne Warner has been that friend for me since 1972. Thank you, Lynne. You know I love you.

Kathleen Schroeder, who makes excellent quilts, has given me good advice and has put things in perspective. She also drives well in the snow. Thanks for all your support while I wrote this book.

American Professional Quilting Systems, Bernina, and Pfaff have very kindly provided me with sewing machines and moral support.

I spent a lot of this last summer at the Baker's Square Restaurant and Pie, in Gurnee, Illinois, at the corner table, near the electrical outlet. While I wrote my book, the staff brought me refills on my soft drinks, sometimes just because the ice had melted. They are so kind to me there.

CHAPTER 1

Boisterous Beginnings

Sneak Peek

In this chapter you'll learn about:

- Colors and Fabrics
- Fused Appliqué
- Free-motion Quilting
- Finishing

*L*ike most people, I started out by making traditional quilts and using traditional techniques, but I soon discovered that this was not my cup of tea. I realized that I really enjoy creating my own designs and developing techniques instead of following someone else's instructions. I always like to be doing something new and different, and that applies to all aspects of my art.

In my early days as a quilter, I came across a catalog from Quilt National, the biennial exhibition that showcases art quilts on the cutting edge. This opened my eyes to the infinite approaches to quiltmaking. During my trips to large quilt shows, I realized that there were many, many ways to make quilts, and all I had to do was find my own path. I began to make my quilts in my own way, with my own voice. This is when I began to love quilting.

Left: "iCandy 2002!" • 2002 • 56" x 69" • This gear design could look like a handful of beads or a garden of flowers. Each circle was made separately, as the whim struck me, then the parts were arranged on a background. Fused appliqué let me cut fused fabric into interesting shapes without worrying about turning edges on points or smoothing the curves.

My style of quiltmaking has evolved from my desire to spend my time on the techniques that enable me to get the designs out of my head and into the cloth quickly. My techniques fly in the face of many of the steps of traditional quiltmaking. But I've enjoyed making every single one of the quilts in this book, because they are designs and techniques that I love to do.

In this book, I am presenting the way I go about making a quilt. Many of my methods came about with input from students and other quilters. Over the years, I've learned as much from teaching as my students have learned from what I have taught. I invite you to try my techniques, even if you think it seems like "cheating" because it is so easy.

Here are some of my methods and techniques:

1. Templates are drawn on paper-backed fusible webbing instead of marking on fabric.

2. Points and edges are matched by laying them down and ironing, instead of precision-piecing a seam.

3. Edges are left raw. I don't spend hours turning them or worrying about folding sharp points.

4. Shapes are fused together, allowing me to use designs that I can't sew together or wouldn't want to hand appliqué.

5. The quilting is unmarked free motion, which lets me get right to the quilting. I'd rather spend the time lavishing the surface with quilting instead of marking, trying to follow a line, and then worrying about whether the markings will wash out.

6. Bindings are fused on; no basting or turning is necessary.

One of the things that makes me the happiest is when a student says, "I never knew it was OK to do it that way. This is *fun!*" Of course, it's OK to do it however you want. There really are no rules for quiltmaking—it's what you make of it.

Colors and fabrics

My methods for choosing colors rely on the theories of contrast, balance, and a few additional guidelines. I don't preplan all the colors of the design before I start cutting fabric. I find that it's easier to pick one shape in the design, choose a color that appeals to me right then, and then pick a second color for the shape next to it that contrasts with the first. Because my designs are simple outline drawings, I make sure that adjacent colors contrast with each other so that the edges of the shapes don't blend together and obscure the design. I move through the quilt, choosing colors for each piece, keeping the concepts of color values, temperatures, and contrasts in mind. I concentrate on one "object" at a time, be it a vase in a still life, a gear, or a guitar. For that object, I limit the color choices to two contrasting colors when possible; using too many colors in each object makes the quilt top an incoherent jumble of color.

CONTRAST

Mixing up color values and temperatures in your quilts will make your piece more interesting and can grab your viewer's attention. Using orange and turquoise against each other will literally make your eyes bounce because you cannot physically focus on both. This adds energy to the quilt as the

robbi's ramblings...

"I consider my quilts 'art' since their purpose is to hang on the wall and give pleasure to the viewer. They are not bed quilts. If a quilt is going to hang on the wall like a painting, it won't need cleaning very often, so leaving edges raw doesn't hurt anything. No one asks how well a watercolor painting will hold up to a good washing. I think of my quilt tops as fabric collage; no one would expect to turn the edges of a paper collage.

In art, you don't get extra points for doing things the long way, and I can't see the point of spending tremendous amounts of time for a result that doesn't matter to me. "

COLOR TIPS

- Using colors that are predominantly warm will add excitement to your quilts. Cool colors will calm them down.

- Using a broad range of values in the design will lend sophistication to the color scheme.

- When you are putting two colors together, move across the room and look at your quilt; this is where a wall that you can pin your work on helps. Make sure you can see the edge of each shape clearly.

BALANCE TIPS

When I have completed two or three shapes, I start paying attention to balance, keeping in mind the following:

- If you use yellow in only one shape in a quilt, that piece will stick out like a caution sign on the road. Use a color in more than one shape.

- Using only one dark shape will make it look like there is a hole in your quilt.

- Using light colors only on one side of the quilt, with dark collecting on the other, will make the quilt look like it's tilting. If I have some yellow on the left side, I use some on the right side to balance it.

- Scatter your colors throughout the quilt, in a triangular fashion. For example, yellow towards the top center, then again on the lower left and lower right. This will give the quilt a sense of balance as well as draw the viewer's eye around the quilt to explore the whole image.

Right: "Groovy Guitars" • 2003 • 40" x 54" • When I choose colors for a puzzle quilt, I let each object "own" a color. For example, the second guitar from the left has an orangey-red fabric in it. On the left side of the quilt, that color only shows up within the boundaries of that guitar. If the same color were used on an adjacent guitar, it would become harder to tell which guitar is which. I used the orangey-red again in another guitar on the right, because it was far enough away.

edges shimmer. For example, look at the orange petals against the blue background in "Fruit and Flowers Emmeshed." Another combination I like to use is lime green against cobalt blue. Both are cool colors, but the lime is warmer than the cobalt, and it has a lighter value too. The colors harmonize because they both have blue in them.

COLOR SCHEMES

The main audience for my quilts is myself, so if the colors make me happy, that is a good color scheme. For an easy color scheme, I often use a triad. For example, below, in "Groovy Guitars," I used three secondary colors: purple, orange, and green. Sometimes I pick only four colors to use. In "Electric Flowers: Summer," I used only yellow, orange, red, and purple, colors that lie alongside each other on the color wheel; blue and green weren't used. "Shoot The Moon" also uses only four colors: blue, yellow, orange, and purple, but no red or green. Sometimes I pick colors that fit a particular mood.

FABRIC COLORS

I love to have many, many choices in color—the more colors the better. To start collecting fabrics to make the quilts in this book, I suggest that you think of going around the color wheel, including yellow, orange, fuchsia, red, purple, aqua, blue, green, and purple. For backgrounds, consider rich neutrals such as a warm brown or a deeper taupe. Create a pile of fabric that looks nice together just as a stack of fabric; if it looks good on your work table, it will look great on your quilt.

"Painterly fabrics" work well for the quilts in this book. Look for tone on tone, imitation hand dyes, and patterns with soft edges or undefined shapes. The viewer should focus on the color of the fabric, not the pictures printed on it. Think of your fabric as woven paint.

Above: This simple six-petal color wheel is all I need to come up with color schemes for my quilts.

Left: "Electric Flowers: Summer" • 2004 • 42" x 52" • This quilt is in a series of "gear" quilts that I designed on the computer. The basic design is the same as in "Shoot The Moon" (page 60), made a year earlier, but I embellished the shapes with small circles to add more detail. The color scheme was simply four colors that are next to each other on the color wheel—yellow, orange, red, and purple—omitting blue and green.

Right: "Fruit and Flowers Emmeshed" • 2005 • 40" x 60" • For this quilt, instead of starting with a specific color scheme, I concentrated on using colors that made me think of a summer garden. The blue background contrasts with the flower petals and evokes a summer sky.

11

HAND-DYED FABRICS

I like working with my own hand-dyed fabrics. Using my own fabrics gives a unique look to my work, and it's a good excuse to keep dyeing fabric, which I find to be pleasurable in itself. I enjoy being able to use colors that appeal to me instead of worrying about what I can purchase. It is also very satisfying to know that the quilt started out with white cloth that I have transformed myself. My dye methods follow my general philosophy of eliminating unnecessary steps and enjoying the fun parts of the process. In Appendix B, you'll find an introduction to dyeing basics and an explanation of my techniques for creating rivers of color.

Fused appliqué

My quilt tops are fused appliqué. In traditional methods of appliqué, shapes are cut out of fabric, the edges are turned, and then the piece is sewn down to a background or another piece, either by hand or by machine. With fused appliqué, I can cut the edges of the fabric exactly to the desired line. The shape is ironed down and attached with fusible webbing onto the background or another piece. I free-motion quilt over all the pieces to hold the quilt top together.

STICK TOGETHER My quilt tops are held together with paper-backed fusible webbing. Think of fusible webbing as a sheet of paper with a heat-sensitive plastic coating of webbing on one side. The webbing side is ironed onto a piece of fabric. The heat melts the plastic enough to make it stick to the fibers of the fabric. When the paper backing is pulled off, exposing the other side of the webbing, the fabric piece can be turned over and ironed onto another piece of fabric. The heat causes the two layers to stick together.

robbi's ramblings...

" *I often use a computer to create the quilt design. I have an engineering background and I take great pleasure from using a high-tech tool to create something of beauty. The contrast between the precision of the shapes drawn by computer and the random beauty of the fabrics appeals to me. It's fun to take advantage of the striations in the fabric to enhance the design, for example, by arranging the stripes to radiate outward in a flower or the cut edge of an orange. See Chapter 3.* "

Left: Detail from "iCandy 2002!"

Right: "King of Cups" • 2000 • 59" x 72" • The outside border was created from a single piece of pour-dyed fabric that I was loathe to cut up into small pieces. I liked the way all the different hues worked together and the dramatic effect of the pattern when the border was mitered. It seemed the perfect way to create a frame for the central image.

Left: "The Moon Hut" • 1995 • 31" x 38" • This is one of my early art quilts. I had read that women are often more creative during their menstrual cycle and wanted a sign for my studio door to warn visitors to leave me alone. The background was made by ironing a solid piece of fusible webbing to a rectangle of orange fabric. I then drew a line on the paper that squiggled all over without intersecting itself, and cut along the line. This gave me two pieces of orange filigree to fuse down onto the pink background. I merely traced around some wooden letters to create the message. To make the objects in the border, I traced around a pair of scissors, my rotary cutter, and a sewing machine logo.

Right: Detail from "iCandy 2002!" • 2002 • 56"x 69" • This a good example of the level of detail you can achieve with fused appliqué. To make it, I used a computer to design the three large flower shapes in the center and for some of the precise flowers surrounding them. For the other circles, I used a regular compass to draw circles of various sizes on fusible webbing. I cut apart the circles and then ironed the circles onto large pieces of hand-dyed cottons. For the smaller flowers, I cut a small circle into a gear or flower shape, and then laid that on top of a larger circle. I kept adding more detail, piling up the flowers. When I felt like I had enough "stuff," I pinned a piece of hand-dyed fabric onto my working wall, and then arranged the flowers on the background until I was delighted with the design. Leaving everything on the working wall, I steam ironed the whole thing to make it stick together. Finally, I trimmed off the parts that stuck out beyond the background.

Full quilt on page 6.

Fused appliqué does have some disadvantages, one of those being frayed edges. This no longer bothers me. I know that the quilt isn't going to continue to unravel, because I heavily free-motion quilt the pieces. I could go back and stitch over the edges by machine, but I don't like the stress of the precision required to follow the edges carefully. It also interferes visually with the hard edge of one shape against another. To keep fraying to a minimum I iron the fusible template onto the fabric leaving a margin, so that I am cutting into fabric that has been bonded on the edges. If the concept of raw edges bothers you, feel free to turn your edges or to cover them with stitches. The techniques and patterns in this book will still be useful to you.

Free-motion quilting

When my quilt top is completed, I use unmarked free-motion machine quilting to hold it all together and to add texture to the surface. I like to do a *lot* of free-motion quilting, so I don't mark the lines ahead of time. With unmarked quilting, I don't have to make decisions about which designs will go in what space before I quilt; I can work intuitively. My creative effort goes immediately into the quilt as opposed to spending time marking the quilt on a flat surface then going back and trying to follow the drawn lines. If there are no drawn lines, I don't have to spend time trying to stay on the exact line when quilting. And if there are no marking lines in the first place, I don't have to worry about getting them to wash out. Ideas for free-motion motifs will come to me as I'm quilting and I am free to try those ideas without having to change a preconceived plan.

Finishing

Most quilters like to cover up the edges of their quilts with a binding. For bed quilts this is an important step that keeps the edges of the quilt itself from fraying in the wash and gives a nice presentation. Since my quilts are hanging on walls, I prefer to fuse strips of binding along the edges and then go back and decoratively stitch over the binding to hold it in place. I think a traditionally stitched binding with turned edges would be inappropriate for a quilt that has raw edges everywhere else. "King Of Cups" was accepted into Quilt National 2001, and that proved to me that fusing was an acceptable way to bind a quilt.

In conclusion, I hope that the ideas in this book will inspire you to grab some fabric and a sharp pair of scissors, and start creating your own art quilts. It's more fun and easier than you can imagine. My wish for my readers is that at some point, you will look at your work and laugh with joy and delight at the results, because the true end result of a quilt is the joy it brings to the artist and the viewer.

CHOOSE TO FUSE

- Fusing lets me have instant gratification. Armed with a line drawing and proposed color scheme, I can start cutting out pieces while an idea is fresh in my mind. Pieces can be up on the design wall in minutes instead of days, and if I don't like the results, I can set a part aside, possibly to be used somewhere else, and choose another color.

- Sections of the quilt can be put up on a working wall and then fused together without having to take them down. Just carry them to a sewing machine, and hope everything stays in the right place.

- I don't have to worry about whether I have the skill to turn the tiny curves, sharp points, and inset corners. With fused appliqué, if you can cut the line, you can use it in your design.

- Fused appliqué is also a good technique to try when piecing a design would require complicated inset corners or an excess number of seams to put a piece in place.

- I like the flatness of fused appliqué. Turned appliqué with a lot of intersections can yield a bumpy quilt surface in all the wrong places. I'd rather add texture with the free-motion quilting or perhaps surface embellishment.

- Working with fused appliqué puts me in a state of right-brained creative flow that isn't interrupted by the left-brained activity of precise stitching.

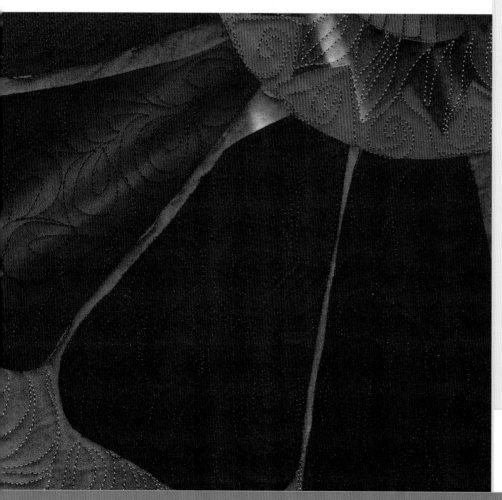

Left and right: Details from "Fruit and Flowers Enmeshed"

CHAPTER 2

Let's Get Started

Many quilters have used fusible webbing in their quilts; it's not a brand new technique. My quilts aren't about the fusing, that's just the technique I use to hold them together until I can quilt them excessively. For me, fusing is the door to exploring designs that I wouldn't attempt if I had to worry about turning a perfect point for hand appliqué or piecing a complicated seam. I've discovered that if a shape can be drawn, it can be fused onto a quilt.

If you keep your eyes open, you will see many opportunities to "choose to fuse" instead of hand appliquéing, or even piecing. The guitar in this sample is a good example of a place to use fusing. Yes, you could turn the edges and hand appliqué all the pieces together. But the neck is so much easier to just iron down onto the front of the guitar instead of trying to turn those corners. Fusing makes easy work of the bridge on the body of the guitar and the circular lines to indicate the sound hole.

Let's go through making a guitar. Making this sample will prepare you for completing a more complicated pattern and designing your own quilt. The pattern for the guitar is on page 114. You can also use the patterns straight out of the book to make a small quilt, or you can blow them up to a larger size. A pattern printed on an 8.5" x 11" sheet will give you a full-sized pattern of 17" x 22". This fits nicely on a fat quarter background.

Sneak Peek

In this chapter you'll learn about:

- **Photographing a subject (a guitar is used as the example in this chapter)**
- **Turning the image into a pattern**
- **Fusing the pattern**

MATERIALS

Guitar quilt label

Paper-backed fusible webbing (¼ yard of 18"-wide webbing or one sheet of 9" x 12" webbing)

Mechanical pencil

Scissors sharp enough to cut fabric fused to paper-backed webbing

9" x 6" scrap of lime green fabric

8" x 2" scrap of violet fabric

8" x 2" scrap of purple fabric

3" x 4" scrap of orange fabric

2" x 2" scrap of red fabric

Optional materials for a quiltlet

18" x 9" piece of background fabric (yellow)

18" x 9" piece of backing fabric (lime green)

18" x 9" piece of batting

18" x 5" piece of fabric for binding

Paper-backed fusible webbing to adhere to binding fabric, either 18" x 5" or 9" x 10"

Left: Simple fused guitar that can be used by itself as a quilt label for the back of a quilt.

Right: Fused guitar used to make a small quiltlet.

Gather your stuff

On the left is the list of what you'll need to make the guitar itself that you could then use as a label if you wanted to. You can use the colors suggested here, or colors of your choice. If you want to make a quiltlet out of the guitar, you will need the additional materials listed under optional materials.

Understanding the pattern

For the guitar pattern, I photographed a guitar and then made a line drawing by tracing the lines in the photograph. If we want the finished guitar to look exactly like the picture, the design for the pattern has to be flipped over. This is because the fabrication process we use will *reverse* the design. When we assemble the guitar, in order to avoid gaps between the pieces, we will overlap adjacent pieces. The overlap is like putting seam allowances on the piece that is underneath. On the pattern pieces, you will see that arrows have been added to the design. The tip of each arrow points to the piece that is laid on top. These arrows will also help you align the pieces.

Figure 1: Photograph of the guitar.

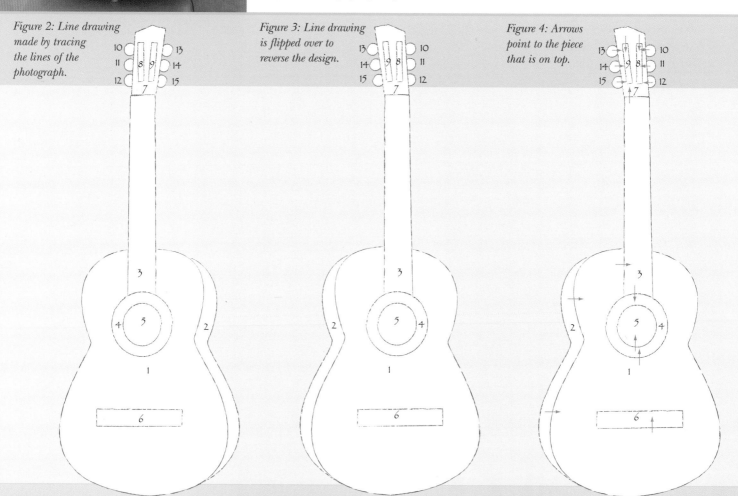

Figure 2: Line drawing made by tracing the lines of the photograph.

Figure 3: Line drawing is flipped over to reverse the design.

Figure 4: Arrows point to the piece that is on top.

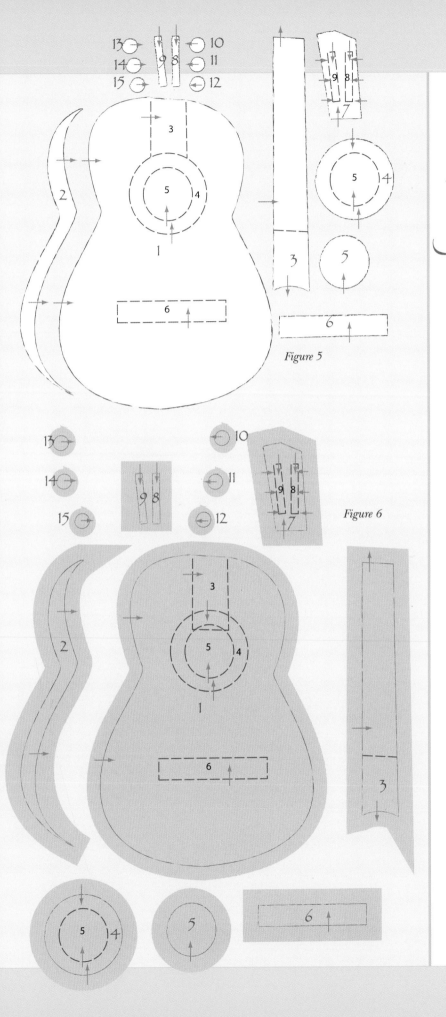

Figure 5

Figure 6

Fusing the guitar sample

1. Copy or reproduce the guitar pattern shown on page 114.

2. Using a sharp pencil, trace around each pattern shape onto the paper side of the fusible webbing. Leave about ½" between each shape so you can easily cut between the shapes.

3. For each pattern piece, copy the piece number (shown in orange) and any dashed lines. The dashed lines will help you position details, such as the sound hole or the guitar neck. The black numbers indicate the piece that will be positioned on the dashed lines. Copy the arrows. Figure 5 shows how your piece of paper-backed fusible webbing should look after you have traced all the shapes in the guitar.

4. Cut out the shapes with a pair of scissors, leaving a ¼" margin around each pencil outline. Figure 6 shows how the templates should look after you have cut them apart.

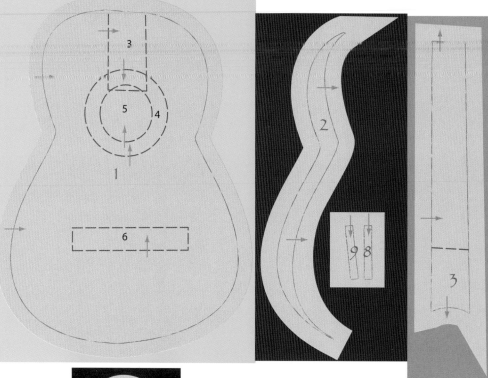

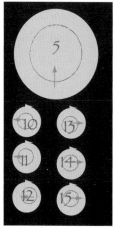

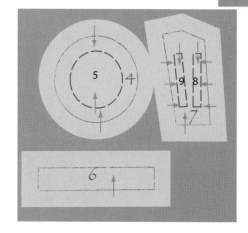

Figure 7

Fusing the guitar sample

COLOR NOTE:

The materials and directions for the guitar sample use the color scheme shown above. If you wish to use a different color scheme, adjust your materials and directions accordingly.

5 Set your iron to dry and press each shape onto the wrong side of the fabric. Then set the iron to steam; flip the piece over and steam press on the fabric side.

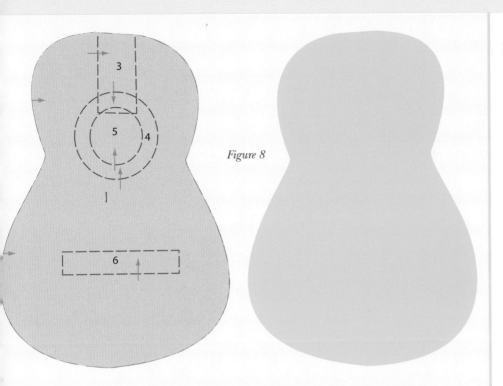

Figure 8

Figure 8 shows what the cut piece looks like on the paper side, and then turned over to the fabric side. Note that the arrows on the left edge have lost the bottom part of the arrow, but the arrow tips are still there. Note also that when you flip the piece over to look at the fabric side, the shape is reversed. Later, when you look at pattern pieces to put them together, make sure you are looking at all of them on the same side, either paper or fabric.

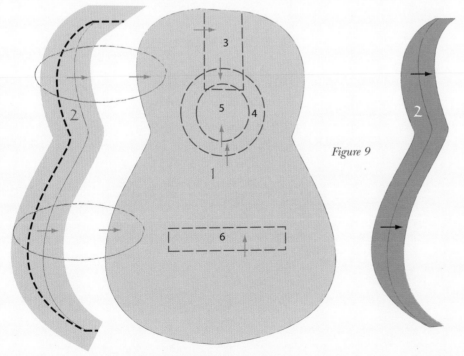

Figure 9

Cut along the heavy dotted line on piece 2.

6 The first piece to cut out is the front soundboard (main body) of the guitar. In order to avoid gaps between the shapes when the guitar is put together, leave a "seam allowance" on one side of each line where the two pieces join. This way one piece can sit on top of the other piece. For example, the guitar soundboard (lime green) will sit on top of the side of the guitar (purple). Remember that the arrows on the patterns point to the pieces that will be on top, and give you a way to align the pieces. Cut out the guitar soundboard neatly, along the outside penciled edge. Leave the paper on.

7 Before you cut out piece 2, the purple guitar side, study it carefully. Do you see that the arrows on the right edge extend out past the edge of the shape? These indicate that you will leave a seam allowance along this edge. These arrows will align with the arrows on the left side of the guitar body. The sets of arrows are circled in orange in Figure 9.

8 Cut out piece 2, cutting along the penciled left edge, but leaving a ¼" seam allowance along the right edge. When piece 2 is cut out, it should look like the one on the right, Figure 9. Here is one way to remember which edges to cut: Don't cut off the tip of the arrows; they indicate the need for a seam allowance. Cut off the legs of arrows; they point to the shape that is on top.

Fusing the guitar sample

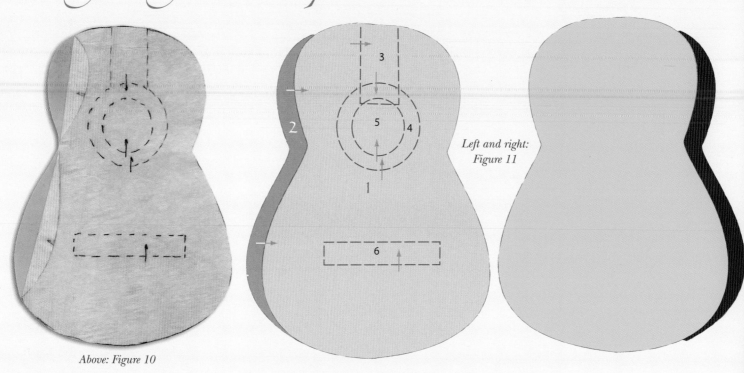

3

2

5 4

1

6

Left and right:
Figure 11

Above: Figure 10

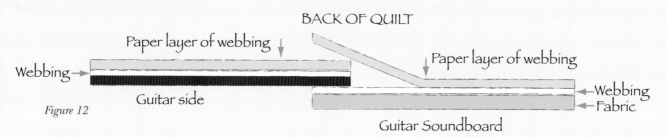

Webbing →

Paper layer of webbing ↓

BACK OF QUILT

Paper layer of webbing

Guitar side

← Webbing
← Fabric

Figure 12

Guitar Soundboard

Figure 11: The guitar on the left shows what it looks like on the paper side, with piece 2 slipped in between the paper and fabric of piece 1. The guitar on the right shows the fabric side, after you have fused the pieces.

Figure 12: This drawing shows a side view of the edge between piece 1, the guitar soundboard, and piece 2, the side. The paper backing on piece 1 has been lifted so the side piece can be slid between the paper and the fabric.

9 Turn piece 1 so you are looking at the paper side. Peel back the paper along the left edge about ½". *(Figure 10)*

10 Slip the right edge of piece 2, the purple guitar side, between the peeled-back paper and the fusible webbing on piece 1. You are essentially slipping the seam allowance of piece 2 in between the paper and fabric of piece 1. *(Figure 12)* Align the arrows on the edges of the pieces. Iron. *(Figure 11)*

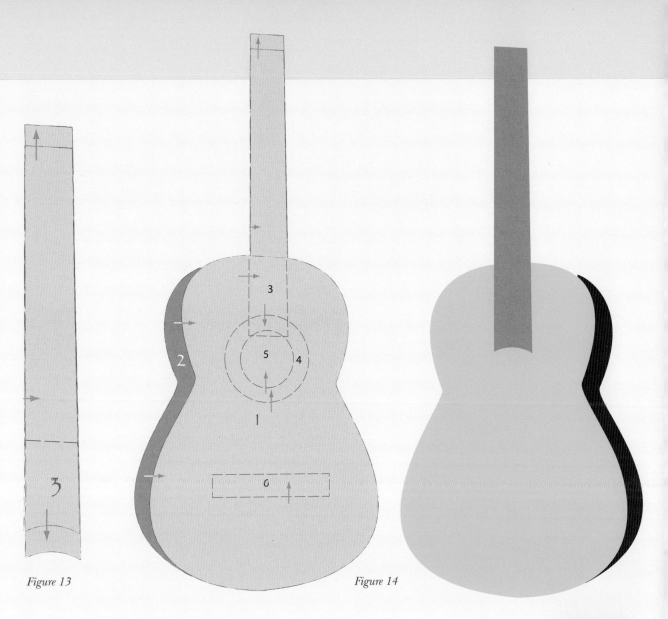

Figure 13

Figure 14

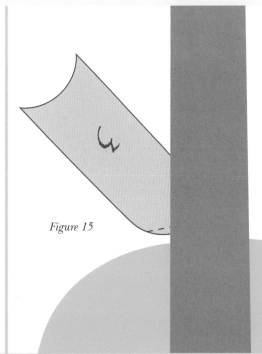

Figure 15

11 Cut out the neck, piece 3. Note that it has seam allowances along the top and bottom edge *(Figure 13)*. The side edges are cut on the penciled lines. The dashed line will help you position the neck on piece 1, the guitar soundboard.

12 Peel apart the paper and fabric on piece 3, the neck, from the bottom up to a little past the dashed line as shown in figure 15. With all paper sides facing you, slip the guitar soundboard, piece 1, in between the paper and fabric of the neck. Use the dashed lines on the guitar soundboard to line up where the neck lies on top of the soundboard. You can hold the pieces up to a light to see the shadow of the neck and make sure it's in the right place. *(Figure 14)*

Fusing the guitar sample

13 Peel the paper off piece 4, the red sound hole. Center piece 4 on top of piece 5, the decoration around the sound hole. If you hold both pieces up to the light, you can use the dashed lines to help you align them. Iron these two pieces together.

14 Peel the paper off piece 5, and lay it onto the guitar, overlapping the base of the neck. Your guitar should now look like Figure 16.

15 Cut out piece 7, the head that is at the top of the neck. Peel apart the bottom edge of the head. Then slip the seam allowance of piece 3, the top of the neck, into the head.

16 Add the rest of the decorative pieces. *(Figure 17)*

17 If you are using the guitar as a small quilt on a background, peel all the paper and iron it onto the background. Free-motion quilting and finishing techniques are covered in the following chapters. *(Figure 18)*

HOT HINTS *for* FUSING

- Use a dry iron on the paper side, steam on the fabric side. This helps avoid bubbles.

- If you are getting bubbles, turn down the temperature on your iron.

- If you still have bubbles, don't worry. Iron hard on the fabric side to squish them down. They won't show up in the finished work.

- Use a quilting pin to separate the paper from the backing. Make a slit in the paper with the pin if necessary, run the pin between the paper and fabric layers.

- Don't leave pins lying around your ironing board. You might accidentally melt a pin into your work. Or maybe it's just me.

- Keep your iron clean so you don't get fusible gunk on the good side of your work.

Figure 16

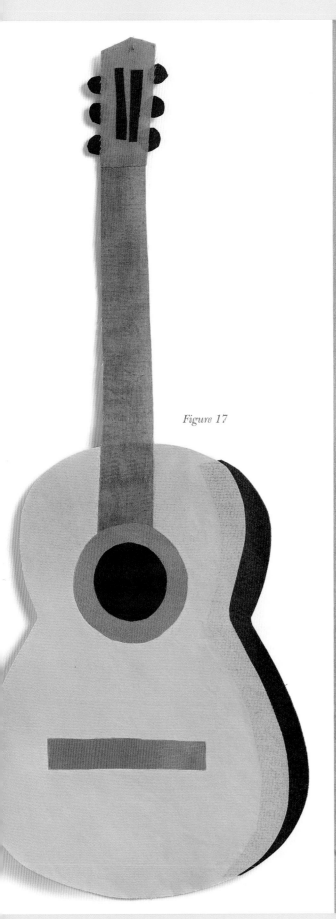

Figure 17

Figure 18

CHAPTER 3

Design Your Own Quilt

When I took a basic color and design class at the local community college, one of our first exercises was to create a collage of interesting objects cut out from magazines. We traced the edges of shapes in overlapping patterns, filling the shapes using only a black pencil. The second exercise was expanded to include black-and-white patterns. The objects the lines represented didn't matter; the shapes were just there to provide boundaries. When we added color theory to the third exercise, we spent weeks gluing down paper cut-outs and creating designs. I realized I could do this with fabric, and I saw quilts waiting to happen. Off I went. That class led to my puzzle quilt series, and then to my still-life series.

Design a puzzle quilt

I've taken numerous drawing classes, and I still can't draw. But I can design and make a beautiful quilt. I'll take you through my process of designing a puzzle quilt. Here are the main steps:

1. Choose the shape of your boundary rectangle.
2. Make a design window.
3. Choose the objects to be included in the design.
4. Trace the objects onto tracing paper.
5. Create a pleasing composition of the objects.
6. Create your final small drawing.
7. Enlarge the pattern to full size.
8. Number the pattern pieces and add construction details.

Left: "Fractal Flowers" • 2001 • 47" x 47" • The design for this quilt was created from free-motion quilting motifs drawn on paper to create a pattern.

Sneak Peek

In this chapter you'll learn about:

- Designing a puzzle quilt
- Designing a still-life quilt
- Designing a quilt from free-motion motifs
- Designing a gear and flower quilt on the computer

HOT HINT

Don't worry about choosing colors for your quilt until you've finished your design and are ready to cut out the pieces. The beauty of fused appliqué is that because it is such an immediate technique, it's easy to change your mind about color choices as you go along. If you don't like a color, you can merely cut out the template with a new piece of fabric. With fusing, you won't spend weeks appliquéing a shape only to discover red would have worked better than purple.

1

CHOOSE THE SHAPE OF YOUR BOUNDARY RECTANGLE

The starting point of my quilt design is choosing the overall shape of the design. In most cases, I am just concerned at this point with the central design. I like to think of the perimeter or boundary of the quilt as a container that I will fill with line and color. For the general shape of the quilt, I often prefer rectangles to squares.

I have found that my puzzle quilts fit in a rectangle with a portrait orientation, while still-life designs seem to fit in landscape formats. Gear quilts and other abstract quilts can fit in either format. For the puzzle quilt in this chapter, I suggest using a boundary rectangle with a portrait orientation.

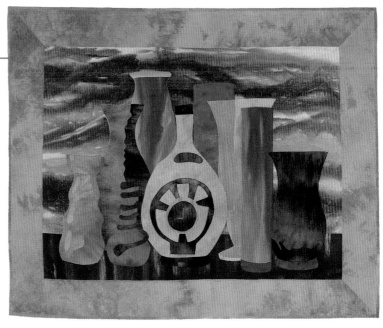

Above: "Borrowed Time" • 66" x 54" • 1998 • This still life of a collection of interesting vases fits well into a landscape orientation.

Above: "Vessels II: The Puzzle" • 30" x 40" • 1997 • The shapes in this puzzle quilt were traced from a collection of magazine pages. The rectangle is a portrait orientation.

Above: "Gears to You" • 41" x 43" • 2003 • In this gear quilt, the big circles as well as some of the smaller ones were designed on the computer. Other patterns were created by cutting, folding, and re-cutting.

A Math Snack

$a \times 1.4 = b$

Let's take a math break, and I'll give you my recipe for the good-looking rectangle I use to size my quilts.

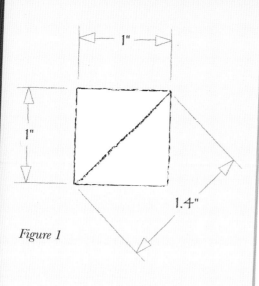

1"

1"

1.4"

Figure 1

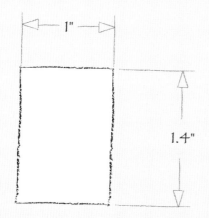

1"

1.4"

Figure 2

We'll start with a short (painless) review of some basic geometry that you'll need to understand. For my quilts, I use a second-degree rectangle, rather than the "golden rectangle" with which you may be familiar. Golden rectangle quilts tend to be much longer in one dimension than the other, while a second-degree rectangle is closer to a square. I think that my rectangles are easier to work with and they make it easier to figure out the quilt size when your design is enlarged.

To construct a proper second-degree rectangle, measure the diagonal of a square that is the same size as the shorter side of the rectangle you are trying to create. So for example, if you are trying to create a quilt with a width of 20", start with a 20" square. The ratio of a proper second-degree rectangle is 1:1.4 (see Figure 2). To create a rectangle using a 20" width, simply multiply 20 by 1.4, and that will give you the length.

These proportions make it easy to see what size your quilt will be when it is enlarged—simply multiply the shorter side by 1.4 to get the length of the longer side.

If all this makes your head hurt, just trust me and remember this:

If you know the shorter dimension, multiply it by 1.4 to get the longer dimension.

If you know the longer dimension, divide it by 1.4 to get the shorter dimension.

Figure 3: Second-degree rectangles in portrait (left) and landscape (right) orientations.

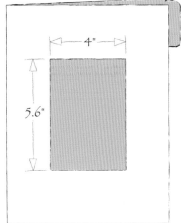

Figure 4

Window cut in left side of folder

Paper taped to inside of right side of folder

Window traced onto the paper

Figure 5

2 MAKE A DESIGN WINDOW

A common manila folder makes a great design tool for puzzle quilts, gear quilts, and quilts with free-motion designs. With a design window, you can easily move around your design elements and then close the window to see how the design will look. I have found that a small window is easier to work with than a larger window. There is less space to fill, so it doesn't seem as daunting. Designs made with a small window can be enlarged to any size you want.

1 On the cover of a plain manila folder, mark a window the same shape as your overall design. To work with a rectangle with a short side of 4", mark a 4" x 5.6" rectangle on the cover (1.4" x 4" = 5.6"). If 5.6" is difficult to measure, go with 5.5" (Figure 4).

2 Cut out the window with scissors or an X-acto knife.

3 Tape a piece of blank white paper to the inside back of the folder to serve as the background sheet. Close the folder and draw the rectangle onto the paper (Figure 5).

3 CHOOSE THE OBJECTS TO BE INCLUDED IN THE DESIGN

You'll need some objects to put in your puzzle quilt. The design lines of your puzzle quilt will consist of simple lines that describe the outline of the objects and perhaps some simple details. You can either take photographs of objects you have laying around your house, find copyright-free photographs you can trace, or go shopping in search of your puzzle items. Don't worry about the size of the image or object because you will adjust the size to fit your design later.

Consider using a minimum of three items to start your design and up to seven for your initial effort. Any more than that and the quilt starts getting very complicated visually, and the parts get small and hard to work with.

HOT HINT If you have a computer, you can scan the tracing and print it out in different sizes on tracing paper or vellum. Use a good quality tracing paper, available at art supply stores. You want tracing paper that is translucent enough to layer four or five sheets and still be able to see the design on the bottom sheet. Drafting vellum is even better; it's easy to see through, stands up to a lot of abuse, and works well in an inkjet printer. (Before running it through a laser printer, check with the manufacturer of the vellum.)

robbi's ramblings...

" *I check out clearance outlets for cheap vases, teapots, teacups, and other kitchen items. I don't care if they are crystal or plastic—I'm looking for shapes and simple lines. I have a $5 rule; if it's under $5, easy to draw, and fairly large, I'll buy it. Chips and flaws don't matter; you can turn them to the back or ignore them. I think of my collection of vases as my 'actors.'*

● *I keep an eye out for interesting magazine photos of common household goods. It is legal to trace a picture of a common teacup for example, as long as you aren't using the composition of the whole photograph.*

● *Look for objects photographed from different points of view, for example, a teacup viewed from above or a vase viewed straight on.*

● *Look for objects that have interesting curved edges that help define the shape of the object. For example, a cup has a rim on the top; tracing around the edge of the rim will show the viewer that it is round. An orange cut in half can show the slices in detail; this will be easier to make it look three-dimensional than the uncut sphere of the orange, which would need shading. A piece of pie is easier to draw than a roll.*

● *Dover Books also has a lot of art you can use, so you don't even have to trace. Look at their coloring books and clip art collections. Check the copyright restrictions listed in the front of their books if you plan to exhibit or publish your work.* "

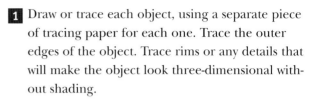

TRACE SHAPES ONTO TRACING PAPER

1 Draw or trace each object, using a separate piece of tracing paper for each one. Trace the outer edges of the object. Trace rims or any details that will make the object look three-dimensional without shading.

2 Once you have traced the object, you can photocopy or scan it and make it bigger or smaller. Your design will be more interesting if you have a good variety of scale to work with. The entire object does not have to fit into the design. In fact, the design will be more intriguing if some of your objects are large and only partially appear in the design.

CREATE A PLEASING COMPOSITION OF THE OBJECTS

1 Open the design window you made and start arranging the cut-out tracings on the background sheet.

2 Using repositionable tape, attach your first object, for example, a vase, to the background. Take a second object; let's say a teapot. Lay it down over the vase, so that the edge of the vase cuts the object approximately in half. Look at the shapes that result from the overlap. Does the edge of the second shape harmonize with the edge of the vase? Slide it around, looking for gentle curves cut out of the vase by the teapot.

3 Add more shapes, keeping in mind the sizes of intersecting pieces that result; avoid having one object just touch the other. Flip some of the objects over to see if their mirror is more interesting.

4 You can either fill the whole picture frame with shapes, or limit the design to a few objects. Remember that you can add shapes later.

Above: "Green Tea" • 65" x 56" •1999 • This quilt is a cross between a still life and a puzzle quilt. The still life was set up, and then multiple pictures taken so that I could trace the edges of all the vessels, whether they were in the front or the back. To create the design, cut-out objects were moved around until the intersecting shapes became interesting. On the left, note the green shape where the vase and the bottle next to it overlap. The blue vase on the far right cuts through the teapot to make an interesting shape. I found that dyed background in my stash; coincidently, it had the greens in the right place to contrast with the orange bulb vase and tall bottle, and the reds to contrast with the blue objects.

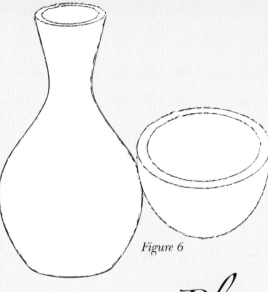

Figure 6

When I start playing with my design for a puzzle quilt, I usually begin by placing a large vase or other simple shape along one side of the rectangle, with some of the vase extending beyond the border of the rectangle on the side and the bottom. A design is more interesting when it engages the edges, instead of having everything floating around in the center of the quilt. With each shape that I add, I experiment with the overlaps, looking at the shapes and edges that result from the overlaps and moving the shapes around.

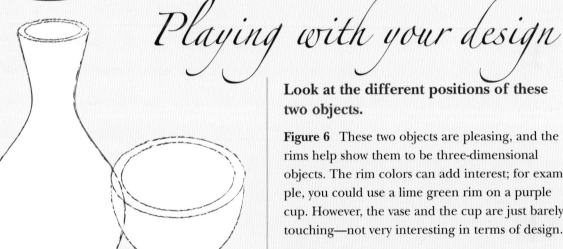

Playing with your design

Figure 7

Figure 8

Look at the different positions of these two objects.

Figure 6 These two objects are pleasing, and the rims help show them to be three-dimensional objects. The rim colors can add interest; for example, you could use a lime green rim on a purple cup. However, the vase and the cup are just barely touching—not very interesting in terms of design.

Figure 7 This design is a little more interesting because the vase and cup have a little bit of overlap. The viewer can ask which object is in front. However, the resulting intersecting spaces are very small and won't be that easy to construct.

Figure 8 This is much better positioning. The right edge of the vase cuts an interesting and graceful line into the cup, and the resulting shapes will be easier to cut out and fuse together.

A note on coloring: Imagine that the vase is blue and the cup is yellow. The overlapping shapes do not have to be green. That would be predictable, and predictable tends to be boring. How about purple? Or red? Use colors that will contrast with the colors next to them, so the viewer can see the lines you are creating.

6 CREATE YOUR FINAL SMALL DRAWING

1 When you are pleased with the design, make sure everything is taped down with repositionable tape to the background paper in your design folder.

2 Either trace the final design on tracing paper or overhead acetate, photocopy it, or scan it, depending on how you plan to enlarge the design to full size in the next step.

7 MAKE A FULL-SIZED PATTERN

We now need a full-sized drawing of your design. You will use this drawing to trace the templates onto the fusible webbing. Remember that this full-sized drawing should be the *opposite* of how you want the final quilt to look, because you will be tracing the templates onto fusible webbing. The webbing gets ironed onto the back of the fabric and then the piece is flipped over. Here are several methods you can use—pick one that suits you.

Method 1 Get a big sheet of paper, or tape several small sheets of paper together, and redraw your pattern full size.

Method 2 Take your pattern to a copy shop and have it enlarged to full size. Some copy shops can also print out your pattern to full size if you have your design on disk as an electronic file. Either use a design created on your computer or scan the drawing. Check first to find out what types of electronic files they can use, and what the maximum size is that they can print.

Method 3 Print out your computer file on the biggest size paper your own printer will take. Tape the sheets together. I got carried away and bought a used inkjet printer that will work with 36" wide paper. Using my wide printer is now my method of choice, because I can make changes and reprint my pattern at 2 A.M. instead of waiting until morning and running to the copy shop.

robbi's ramblings...

...What size should the quilt be?

Because the ultimate goal for most of my quilts is to submit them to quilt shows, I often am making a quilt with a specific show's deadline and rules in mind. In truth, I usually have more than one show in mind when I start a quilt, since I don't want to make one quilt for every show. You may think this is a crass way of doing things, but I need to have a goal and a deadline when I start a quilt. I'm one of those people who can manage to take all allowable time to finish a task, because when faced with too many choices, I can't make up my mind. Show requirements help me narrow down all the possibilities for size, and a deadline keeps me from spending months on a minor design point.

If you don't have a particular show in mind, or are making something to hang on your wall, consider using the width of your background fabric as a starting point. For example, let's assume you have a 40" width of muslin for the background for a puzzle quilt. Using my preferred proportion of 1 to 1.4, a design that is 40" wide would be 56" long. You could then sew borders onto that piece of fabric, making the quilt bigger if necessary.

The nice thing about art quilts is that they don't have to fit on a bed, so you can use any size you want. In my workshops, we use 18" x 22" as the size of the design. Why? Because 18" is the maximum size roll of paper I can fit on my carry-on when I fly to teach, and it fits nicely on a fat quarter of background fabric.

Method 4 Manually trace your design from your design window onto clear acetate. Then project it full size using an overhead transparency projector. Use a large sheet of paper to trace the projected design, or tape sheets of poster board together. The poster board makes a good base to draw on; you can fold it up along the edges for storage. If you have a scanner, you can scan your design and run the transparency sheet through your printer; both inkjet and laser versions are available. You can also take your design window to a copy shop and have them transfer it onto an acetate transparency for you. If you have your own photocopier, you can do this yourself.

Method 5 If you have access to a full-sized opaque projector (the kind used in schools), trace the design or print it out on white paper and project it onto paper or poster board. There are some small, inexpensive opaque projectors on the market, but the problem with this size projector is that the original image usually has to be small, about 4" x 5" maximum, and the light isn't bright enough to see unless the room is completely dark.

8 NUMBER THE PIECES AND ADD CONSTRUCTION DETAILS

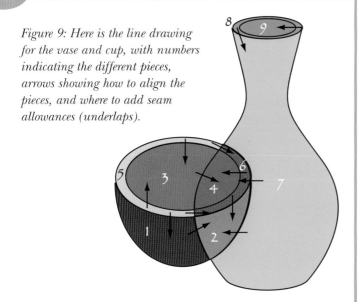

Figure 9: Here is the line drawing for the vase and cup, with numbers indicating the different pieces, arrows showing how to align the pieces, and where to add seam allowances (underlaps).

Figure 10: Here is the line drawing for the vase and cup with numbered parts. Pieces 1 and 2 make up the body of the cup, 3 and 4 make up the inside of the cup, and 5 and 6 indicate the rim. Pieces 2, 4, and 6 are also part of the vase body and pieces 7, 8, and 9 show the vase body, rim, and inside.

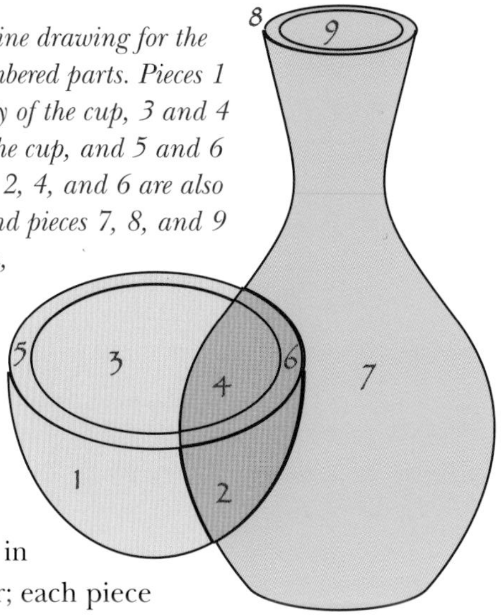

1 Number your pattern pieces. The numbers don't have to be in any special order; each piece just needs its own number.

2 Remember those arrows we used in Chapter 2 to indicate how to overlap the pieces? We'll begin to add those now. Wherever the edges of two pieces meet, one has to be on top, the other on the bottom, with an overlap (seam allowance). I like to make the edges that define the shape of an object be on top. To show that on my design, I use highlighting markers in different colors. So, in this example, I drew a yellow line just inside the outline of the body of the cup (pieces 1 and 2) to show that these pieces will go on top of the background and the vase, respectively (Figure 11). Note that the colored line is drawn just inside the black line, not on top of it. Together, pieces 3 and 4 define the inside of the cup, so I drew an orange line just inside the black oval that outlines those pieces.

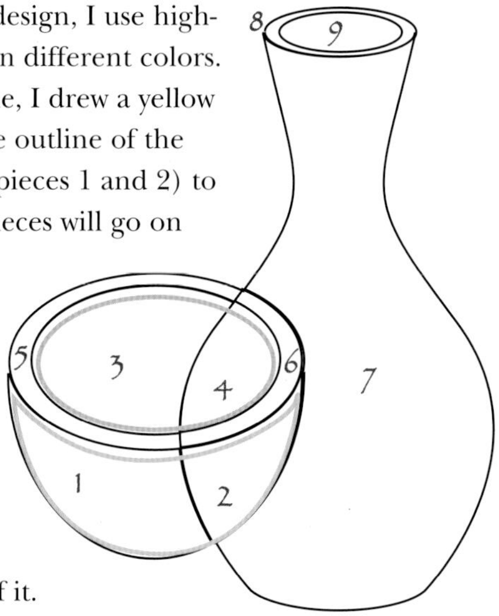

Figure 11

3 Now, in some cases, one side of a piece will be on top and the other side will be underneath another adjoining piece. That's the case in pieces 5 and 6 that make the rim of the cup. Because the upper edges of the pieces lay on top of the background (piece 5) and the vase (piece 6), but the lower edge of the pieces will go under pieces 1 and 2, we are going to highlight only the upper edges of pieces 5 and 6 (Figure 12). Remember, the black outlines can have highlighter on only one side, because one piece has to go on top (the highlighted side) and one piece has to go under (not highlighted).

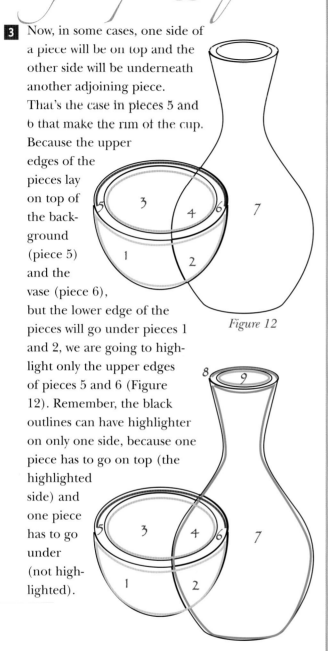

Figure 12

Figure 13: Here, all the highlighted lines have been drawn. Note that because the top of the vase rim lies on top of the background while the lower half lays beneath pieces 9 and 7, the purple highlight line is drawn only on the top half of piece 8.

4 Once your pieces are highlighted, add arrows that point to the piece that is on top. The arrows also act as alignment marks. The arrow should start on the side of the line that has no colored highlighting (the piece that will be going underneath) and stop on the part of the piece that will be on top (highlighted). Remember, the arrows point to the edge of the piece that will go on top. (Figure 14)

5 Make your templates, copying arrows onto all the pieces so you can use them to line up the parts. Figure 15 shows the individual pattern pieces, or templates, with the arrows. You don't need to copy the colored lines onto the template; they are shown here to tell you what the lines do.

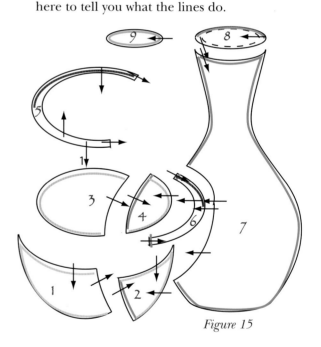

Figure 14

Figure 15

Congratulations! You've created a design for a puzzle quilt using a design window, you've made a full-size pattern, and you've marked all of the construction details on the pattern pieces. Your next step is to choose fabric colors for your design. After that, you can get started on putting the quilt top together.

CONSTRUCTING THE TOP

The full details for constructing the top are given in Chapter 2, but here is a brief summary of how you will put the top together.

1. Trace each template on fusible webbing, leaving a margin around each shape. Your templates should look like the ones in Figure 15.

2. Cut apart the templates, leaving a margin around all edges.

3. Iron the fusible onto the wrong side of the fabric.

4. Cut out the fabric piece.

   a. If there is no arrow along the edge or the arrow points into the piece, cut along the black line.

   b. If the arrow points out along that edge, leave a margin in the fabric. A way to remember this is that you never want to cut off the arrow heads.

5. Slip the margins in between the fabric and paper layer of the fusible, aligning drawn edges and the arrows. Press using steam.

6. Peel off all the paper when you are done. Put the fabric on a background.

CHOOSING FABRIC COLORS FOR PUZZLE QUILTS

In order for the viewer to discern the objects you are depicting in the quilt, they must be able to clearly see the outline of each object. The design lines are easier to see if the shapes on either side of the line contrast with each other. You can contrast the colors either by value (for example, light blue against dark blue), or with temperature (yellow, a warm color, next to blue, a cool color). Yellow next to purple gives you both value and temperature contrasts. I usually assign a color to an object; for

example, the vase "owns" blue, and the cup "owns" red. Wherever the vase is shown, without any other overlapping object, it will be blue. However, if I need to change the color for the rim, then I pick a third color for that, for instance, green.

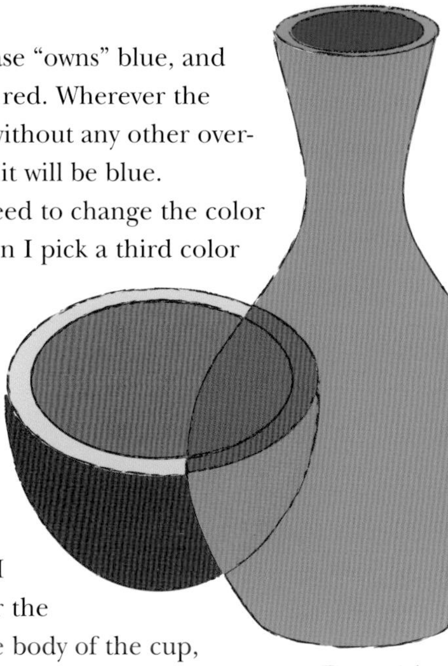

Figure 16 shows a possible coloring of our vase and cup. Note that I used orange for the right half of the body of the cup, instead of using purple, which you would get if you mixed red and blue paint. I thought it would be interesting if that part were orange. Keep in mind that these objects aren't really overlapping, they are just a design. You can put whatever color looks good wherever you want.

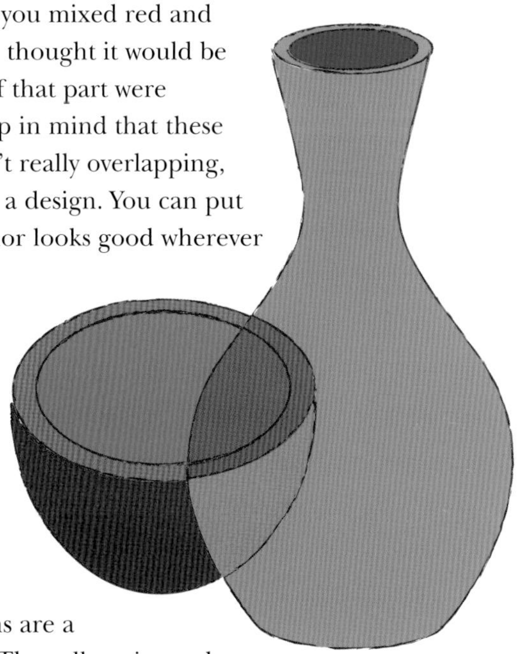

Figure 16

Figure 17 shows another coloring. I have issues with this one. First, these color combinations are a little bland. The yellow rim and orange interior in Figure 16 are punchier. Second, the interior of the cup in Figure 17 is blue, as is the vase. This can confuse the viewer. If you use blue for the body of the vase, keep the blue within the outline of the vase, as shown in Figure 16.

Figure 17

robbi's ramblings...

" *In my still lifes, I like to include objects that have sentimental value or tell a story. I've used a bottle clock given to me by my grandmother, her pearls, as well as vases given to me by a friend and a teapot found in the attic of another friend. I always imagine a 'scene' for the still life, as it gives a story and meaning to the objects. In 'Half Past Midnight,' I pretended it was right after celebrating New Year's Eve as the millennium turned. I included a wine glass from the celebration, my grandmother's pearls, a clock, and a coffee cup tipped over after too much celebrating. In 'Tea and Empathy,' I thought about lunches with my friend Lynne. After 30 years, she knows me better than anyone else, and I can discuss any problem with her. We share our troubles, laugh at each other and ourselves, and always feel better at the end of the meal—even if we haven't solved the problem. I wanted to make a quilt to honor how lucky I am to have such a lifelong friend. For this still life, I used bagels and teapots instead of lunch items because I was picturing the two of us sitting somewhere in the morning having a lovely chat. Lynne gave me the bulb vase, thinking it would be an interesting addition to one of my quilts, so I used that vase along with a large yellow vase I bought at an outlet store, intrigued by its interesting top edge and stripes.* "

Left: "Still Life with Strawberries" • 2001 • 62" x 62" • I bought the pitcher and plate the day my daughter graduated from 8th grade; the wine bottle was from the Quilt National 2001 opening; and my friend Lynne gave me the mirror just to put in a still-life quilt. It's nice to look at the objects and remember where they came from. I arranged the objects with the tallest towards the back, the shortest in the front. The top of the bottle and the cup on the right form another triangle, a device to create a composition.

Design a still-life quilt

The still life has been used as subject matter for artwork for centuries and in just about any art form you can think of—drawings, paintings, mosaics, collages, and of course quilts. A trip to the local library or bookstore should yield a large selection of books about still lifes in various media. Look in books collecting works by specific painters to see how they approached a still life. It's especially enlightening to look at the art of Cézanne, who was known for his magical still lifes, as well as other post-Impressionist painters. Books on painting still lifes with watercolors will have information that can easily be applied to art quilts, especially theories about composition.

The beauty of a still life is that, by definition, the objects don't move. Even if you can't draw, you can photograph objects arranged on a table and then trace the edges in the photo to get your line drawing. This is not cheating: this technique has been used since the Renaissance when camera obscuras were used by painters.

Here are the main steps for designing a still-life quilt:

1 Choose the objects in the still life.

2 Create a pleasing composition of the objects.

3 Create a line drawing.

4 Choose a boundary for the design.

5 Enlarge your design to the size of the quilt.

6 Add construction details to the pattern.

7 Enlarge the pattern to full size.

1 CHOOSE THE OBJECTS IN THE STILL LIFE

Choose a theme for your still life, such as objects that are similar (for example, several vases or bottles, kitchen utensils, or gardening tools) or relating to a person (perhaps things related to a favorite sport or hobby).

2 CREATE A PLEASING COMPOSITION OF THE OBJECTS

Still-life composition alone can take up a whole book. So briefly, here are some steps to get you started with your composition.

1 Choose a place to arrange your still life. Use a simple background and table surface to make it easier to see what you have. Also, consider the color of the background and table compared with the color of the objects; it's easier to trace edges when the shapes contrast with the background. Remember—you can make the background any color you want when you start working with the fabric.

2 Place the tallest object towards the back with shorter objects in the front, like a class picture. Arrange the peak of the tallest object off center, to give your composition the shape of a triangle.

3 Overlap the objects in an interesting fashion. Look at the negative space left between the objects.

4 If you use objects with handles (teapots, cups, etc.), consider where the handle points. A cup handle pointing back to the center of the composition will draw the viewer's eyes away from the edge. Knives, spoons, and forks can also guide the eye.

5 If you are using a mirror, look into it as you set up your composition. Don't position an object so its reflection is exactly behind it because it will be hard to distinguish the real item from the reflection. Keep in mind that what's in the

robbi's ramblings...

" *A digital camera is really useful for creating a line drawing; even an inexpensive digital camera with low resolution is very useful. I set up my digital camera on a tripod and take pictures, moving the objects around. Take pictures from various points of view, higher and lower. A higher point of view will make it easier to trace the edges of your items and make them look three dimensional without a lot of shading. The camera's flash will create odd shadows, but since I don't use shadowing or shading in my designs, this doesn't bother me. But I do take two pictures of each composition—one with flash, one without—from the same position, as sometimes details will be easier to see in one photograph than the other. Then I transfer the images to my computer so I can look at them on a larger screen and see what I have. I can go back and retake pictures until I have one I like.*

If you don't have a digital camera, shoot a roll of regular film, moving the objects around and using different points of view. "

HOT HINT Many computer applications made to process photographs have a tool that can be used to trace the edges of an object in a photo. For example, in Adobe Photoshop, go to Filter-Stylize-Find Edges. This tool will almost make the drawing for you. You will have to ignore some of the extra lines and add detail, but it's a great shortcut that you can use with a digital image.

mirror does not have to be what's in front of the mirror. You can use two compositions, one in front, and one behind. Remember this is art, not journalism.

TIPS *for* TREASURE HUNTING

- ◉ I keep an eye out for objects that have interesting shapes and edges that can easily be traced when photographed.

- ◉ I don't use flowers, because I find them too complicated to work with. If this is not the case for you, treat yourself to some lovely fresh flowers, or even silk imitations.

- ◉ I like to use vases because they come in all kinds of materials and often have gentle curves. I like to collect them and buy them with the excuse that they could end up in a quilt.

- ◉ Teapots work well with vases, as they are short and often round, a nice complement to tall, skinny vases. You can ignore small details in objects.

- ◉ The real color of an object doesn't matter: once you have the line drawing, you can make that vase any color you like.

- ◉ The condition of the object doesn't matter either. I bought a teapot and coffee pot that both had cracks. The antique dealer sold them very cheaply, because they weren't worth anything as collectibles due to their condition.

- ◉ Outlet stores, garage sales, and your friends' cupboards are good places to look. My friends give me things to put in my still lifes when they find something they think I will enjoy. I like to use these, because they remind me of the friend.

- ◉ Using food is fun. Slice up an orange, an apple, or throw a piece of toast on a plate.

- ◉ Add a spoon somewhere and you will make the viewers feel that they can reach into your still life and pick it up.

- ◉ Small mirrors can make the still life more interesting, too. Consider changing the color of an object when it is reflected in a mirror. For example, the teapot on a table can be orange, and its reflection blue. It's art.

CREATE A LINE DRAWING 3

1 Once you are pleased with the composition of your still life, draw the design or take photographs with a traditional or digital camera.

2 When you have a picture you like, print it out on a full sheet of paper; it is easier to work with a large copy of the picture than a tiny one. If you used a regular camera, you can take the print into a copy shop and have it enlarged to 8" x 10" on a photocopier. You can also have a film developer transfer your pictures into a digital file and print it out in a larger size.

3 Turn the picture into a line drawing. Using a sheet of good quality tracing paper, trace the edges of all the objects. Include detail lines that help make the object look more real. You can exaggerate the rim of things. Don't worry about perfection; if you pay attention to graphic art outside of quilting, you will see that people draw things very oddly all the time.

CHOOSE A BOUNDARY FOR THE DESIGN 4

Now you need to determine the boundary of your drawing. There are several ways to do this.

Method 1 Cut two sheets of paper into L-shapes and move them around, framing your design. When you find a pleasing boundary, transfer this to the tracing paper.

Method 2 If you have a computer, scan the drawing. Then, open it in a graphics file and crop the design to your heart's content.

Method 3 You can use the design window explained in the puzzle quilt section of this chapter. You may want to make a bigger window or reduce the size of the drawing to fit into the window.

From this point on, you can follow the directions for the puzzle quilt at the beginning of this chapter, starting with step 6 on page 36.

Design a quilt from free-motion motifs

Free-motion quilting motifs drawn out on paper can be an excellent source for designs for the quilt top itself. My first quilt of this type came about during a watercolor painting class when I couldn't think of what to paint. I started scribbling on watercolor paper until I got a design I liked, painted it, and then realized it could be enlarged for a quilt design.

Start by filling sheets of paper with free-motion quilting design motifs, varying the motifs as you would on a large section of a quilt. Use the design window to pick a section of the page that looks interesting. Then photocopy or trace it, and color it in. You may need to add more lines to divide the design space.

Once you have a design you like, enlarge it to make the pattern for the quilt. One thing I like about this type of design is that you can then free-motion quilt it, using the same motifs within each design area.

Above: "Electric Flowers, Night" • Detail • I lined up all the petal templates to run with the grain of the dyed fabric, so that the cut-out petals look like they are radiating out from the center of the flower.

Designing a gear and flower quilt on the computer

I designed my gear and flower quilts on the computer, using a graphics application called Canvas. Canvas runs on both the Windows platform and the Macintosh operating system. Corel Draw and Adobe Illustrator are similar software programs.

Most drawing programs have tools for making squares, rectangles, spirals, and stars. The fun part of using a computer is that you aren't limited to using 8- or 16-pointed stars. If you want a star with 22 points, just tell the computer to make it for you.

Right: "Electric Flowers, Night" • 2004 • 42" x 54" • This gear quilt was designed on the computer. The templates were printed out by running Wonder-Under fusible webbing through an ink-jet printer.

Figure 18 The stars in the top row were drawn just using the star tool. In the bottom row, stars were drawn with the "smooth" option selected.

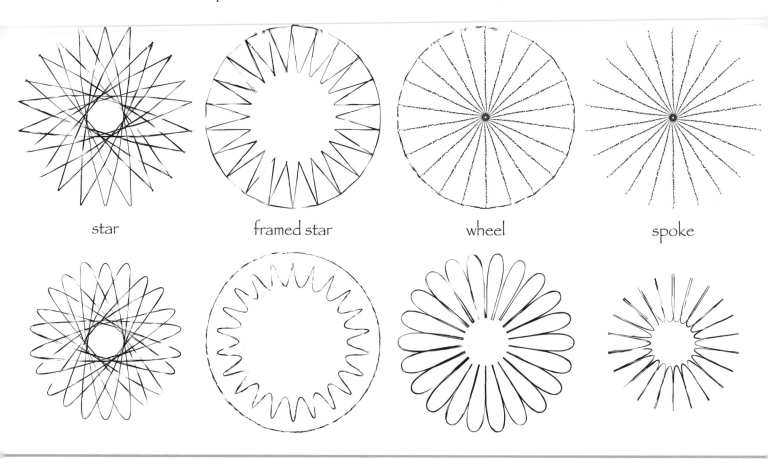

star   framed star   wheel   spoke

Figure 19 First, a wheel was drawn with the star tool, with smoothing turned on. Next, a circle was drawn. Then, the two shapes were aligned to create a flower.

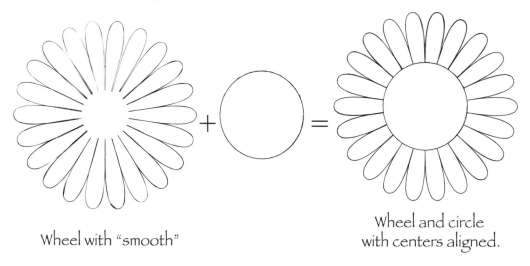

Wheel with "smooth"

Wheel and circle with centers aligned.

Right: "Electric Flowers, Summer" • 2004 • 42" x 52" • This gear quilt is the same design as "Shoot the Moon," but with a different color scheme and further embellishment of the petals. Using the "smooth" command gave me flowers; turning it off yielded the stars. The pointy star in the lower right came from a framed star, as shown in Figure 18, second from left in the top row. The same star when "smoothed" yielded the gear shape on the lower left of the quilt. The flowers were all designed using the star tool, resizing and stacking them as in Figure 19. The smaller circles were cut with a Sizzix Die Cutter.

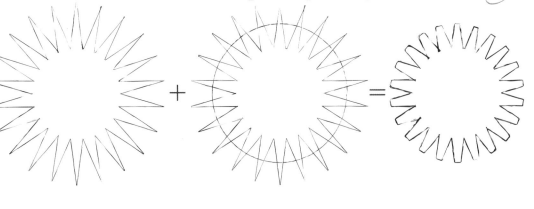

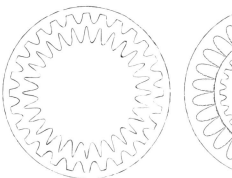 +  =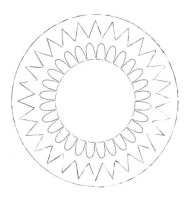

Figure 20 Create a star with blunted tips. First, draw a star and then a circle. Align the centers of the two shapes. Cut off the tips using the "combine" tool, set to "divide."

Figure 21 More flower and gear shapes combining stars.

Figure 22 A whole quilt design using computer-generated designs.

Giving you complete directions for designing quilts on a computer could be a very thick book in itself, as the possibilities are endless. If you want to give computer-generated designs a try, my advice is to download one of the many trial versions available on the Web, and start to play. Many community colleges have introductory courses on how to use graphic applications. Also, you can try one of my own computer-generated patterns found in Appendix A.

Left: "Gears to You" • 2003 • 41" x 43" • The star tool was used extensively to design this quilt, but with only one large overlapping circle. To fill out the rest of the surface, I carried precut circles around with me and made flowers when I had free time. The blunted "gear shapes" on both quilts were made by cutting off the tips of the stars and flowers. Once I get a shape I like, I can make them bigger and smaller and stack them up to get infinite possibilities of flowers and gears.

Free-motion Quilting

Sneak Peek

In this chapter you'll learn about:

- Setting up your machine and test stitching
- Free-motion quilting motifs
- Showing off with variegated threads, programmed stitching, and twin needles
- Quilting the "real" quilt
- Batting and fusing

I love the process of free-motion quilting. I make myself comfortable, put on a pair of headphones, and lose myself in it. I work on small sections at a time, considering only what section is in front of me, taking in the beauty of the fabric and the shape of the specific piece, and watching what emerges from the needle. Free-motion quilting puts me in a state of flow, and I lose track of time and my surroundings.

I free-motion quilt pretty excessively—the lines are usually about a quarter inch apart, sometimes even closer. I allow about an hour per square foot of quilt, including changing thread, keeping the machine clean, doing the actual quilting, and, very rarely, ripping out stitches. I like to have a lot of quilting on a piece because it adds a second layer of design, one that I hope pulls the viewer closer and entertains them by presenting something new to look at in each section of the quilt.

robbi's ramblings...

" *The term 'free-motion quilting' means that you will be controlling the direction and length of the stitches. The machine will move the needle up and down for you, but you will move the quilt back, forth, and sideways. Think of the machine as the pencil, and you are moving the paper. For some beginners, this whole idea is nerve wracking, but I'm here to tell you that it's not so hard once you get the hang of it.* "

My free-motion quilting designs consist of motifs that are generally about 1" square, with a different motif being used in each fused shape in the quilt. More complex motifs, such as flowers, are slightly larger and are created by combining smaller motifs. In this chapter, I'll introduce the basics for several different motifs, and then show you how to vary and combine them.

Left: "One Last Orange" • 53" x 71"

EQUIPMENT AND SUPPLIES

Sewing machines

Any sewing machine in good working order can be used for free-motion quilting, from the most basic machine that will only straight stitch to the fancy top-of-the-line machines. Here are some basic tips for getting your sewing machine ready for free-motion quilting.

1   **Have a machine in good working condition.**
    This is the most important first step in free-motion quilting. On a regular basis, you should take your machine into a dealer and have it cleaned, oiled, and adjusted for you. Machines build up lint in areas you can't reach yourself, and interior parts can get loose. Do yourself a favor and have your machine serviced before you start a new project.

2   **Know how to set up your machine properly, and know how it works.**
    For free-motion quilting, you need to know how to set up the machine, including dropping the feed dogs, adjusting the needle tension, changing the needle, choosing needle stop up/down if that's an option, changing the stitch plate if you have an extra one, winding a bobbin, and cleaning, oiling, and installing the bobbin case.

3   **Start off with the right foot.**
    The regular foot that you use for sewing seams won't work for free-motion quilting because it won't hop up out of the way when you need to move the quilt. You need a foot that has a spring or lever in the shank to let it hop up. Most machine manufacturers offer a quilting foot specifically made for free-motion quilting. It's similar to a darning foot except usually the shoe is bigger; often they are made of clear plastic, making it easier to see what you are doing. The larger opening of the foot will also allow you to use zigzag and decorative stitches for your free-motion quilting.

If you have a really old machine and you can't find a darning foot or a quilting foot, buy a spring needle. It's just a needle mounted on a spring. There are a few drawbacks to the spring needle. First, it has a white piece of plastic holding the needle in place. The white piece bobs up and down with the needle, which makes my eyeballs bounce. Also, it's nice to have a little bit of foot to protect your fingers.

EYE PROTECTION If you wear glasses, keep them on during free-motion quilting because needles can break and parts can fly around. Consider safety glasses or goggles if you still have perfect eyesight, so that it stays that way.

4   **Use a straight stitch plate if you have one.**
    The stitch plate is the metal or plastic part that covers the bobbin area. It has a hole for the needle to pass through during stitching, a hole that is normally wide enough to allow the needle to swing sideways during zigzag or decorative stitching. Machines that can only do a straight stitch have a stitch plate with a small circular hole, since the needle doesn't have to move side to side. The larger opening in a zigzag machine doesn't support the quilt as well during free-motion quilting as the stitch plate with the smaller hole; skipped stitches can result. Most machines that do zigzag stitching can also be fitted with an optional straight stitch plate that has the small round opening. If you have a straight stitch plate, try it with your free-motion quilting and see if it makes a difference. The bigger holes can also eat the leading edge of your fabric if you are piecing a skinny quilt patch. Remember that when you are using a straight stitch plate, don't switch to zigzag or decorative stitching or move the needle off center—you'll break a needle. If you are having skipped stitches but don't have a straight stitch plate, consider moving the needle all the way to the right or left if you have that feature on your machine—this will help support the quilt better.

Sewing surface

It's important to support the entire weight of the quilt at the same level as the machine bed. If the quilt is pulling against the needle, the needle will bend or bang against the stitch plate and break. I work on a very small area, starting in the center of the quilt. I keep my machine in a cabinet, and the machine is lowered so that the machine bed is even with the level of the cabinet. A table to the left of the cabinet supports the weight of the quilt on that side of the machine and either an extension of the cabinet or a separate table sits behind the machine to support the quilt behind the machine. A sturdy cabinet will keep the machine from bouncing up and down while the machine is running at full speed.

Needles

Schmetz makes an embroidery needle that is excellent for free-motion quilting with most threads. I try to use the smallest needle that will smoothly pierce the surface of the quilt without shredding the thread, which is usually a Schmetz size 75. I use the size 12 Coated Titanium Sharp needle made by Organ. The needles were originally designed for the commercial embroidery industry where broken needles or thread would slow down production. The coating on the needle is perfect for free-motion quilting on fused quilts because it enables the needle to slide through the fabric more easily. Titanium needles wear down more slowly than regular needles. A needle with a worn tip will cause skipped stitches. Titanium needles are expensive, so when you are first getting comfortable with free-motion quilting, you may want to stick with less expensive needles.

Schmetz also makes twin embroidery needles in several styles. These can be used in free-motion work and add extra interest to the surface.

Thread

I will freely admit to being a thread junkie. Just as most quilters want a big stash of fabric, I want a big stash of thread with lots of colors and styles. Most of the threads I use are referred to as machine embroidery thread, usually 40 weight. In addition to solid colors, threads can be variegated, which means that one spool has sections of different shades of the same hue, or different colors altogether.

Polyester embroidery thread is stronger than rayon, holds up better in washing, is lightfast, and is more resistant to shredding, which makes it my choice when using solid color threads. I prefer Madeira Polyneon or Isacord, and both come in a myriad of colors. While Isacord is currently only available in solids, Madeira makes a variegated line of polyester threads. Superior also makes a beautiful line of variegated thread in spools that stand up on their own and have shorter sections of each color.

Rayon embroidery thread is not as strong as polyester, so I only use rayon when it has a variegated thread that I can't find in polyester. Some of the brands I use are Madeira, Sulky, and FuFu.

Metallic threads often shred faster, but using needles specifically made for metallic threads and topstitching can minimize this. I have used Madeira, Yenmet, Sulky, and Superior metallic threads with success.

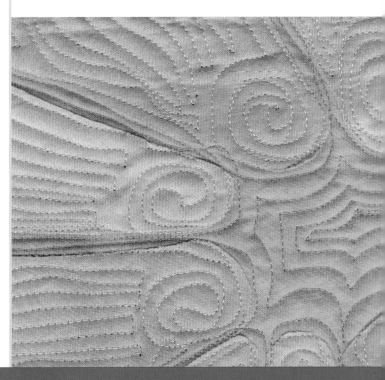

BOBBIN THREAD

Some people match the bobbin color to the backing fabric, but I prefer to consider what color thread is being used in the needle. No matter how well your tension is adjusted, you will still see the bobbin thread on the front of the quilt; it's part of the stitch being formed. For example, if you have used black thread to match the backing fabric, and the top is a light color, you'll see little dots of black on the front. Or vice versa. Since you spend more time looking at the front of the quilt, it should be the more important factor in choosing threads. The color changes that occur on the back of the quilt lend an extra design element to the quilt, and the lines of the stitching on the back can be appreciated. It always thrills me when someone sees the back of a folded up quilt and compliments me, thinking it's the front. I prefer to use my hand-dyed fabrics on the back of the quilt, but if you want to make an attempt to hide your stitching, use a very busy print made up of two highly contrasting colors. It's harder for the eye to focus on the stitches while being distracted by the print.

Here are some rules of thumb I use to pick bobbin threads:

- With a solid color needle thread that matches the color of the backing fabric, use the same solid in the bobbin.

- With a solid color needle thread that contrasts with the backing fabric color, match the bobbin thread to the fabric. The line looks smoother.

- With variegated rayon or polyester needle threads, choose solid polyester bobbin thread that coordinates with one of the colors in the needle thread. For example, if you are using a variegated needle thread that has four shades of blue, you could use a light blue or medium blue for the bobbin.

- With metallic needle threads, use a polyester solid in the bobbin to match either the top thread or the backing fabric.

TEST STITCHING AND PRACTICING

I always practice on a few pieces of felt or sample quilt sandwiches before I start working on my main quilt. This allows me to test my threads, fine tune the tension, and get my quilting muscles warmed up. Two felt squares layered together make an excellent practice material. Felt squares provide enough body to grab, they are cheap enough to treat as "scratch paper," and they don't require any advance preparation. You don't have to baste the test sandwiches.

Setting up your machine for test stitching

1 **Drop the feed dogs.** I prefer the feed dogs down so they don't drag on the quilting, but some people prefer them up. On some machines, it's easier to install the free-motion foot when the feed dogs are lowered. If you can't drop the feed dogs, set the stitch length to zero.

2 **Insert a new needle.** If free-motion quilting is new to you and breaking expensive needles is a concern, just use a regular universal needle while you practice the motifs. If the thread starts shredding, change to one of the embroidery needles. A size 80 or 90 is good to start with for a universal needle; start with the 75 if you are using a Schmetz embroidery needle. Remember that titanium needles are expensive, and they don't bend as easily—better to break an inexpensive needle than bang up your machine with titanium.

3 **Pick a thread to use in the needle.** Your practice stitching will look nicer if the thread matches the material, but if you want to see what you are doing, use a contrasting color. Just keep in mind that on your real quilt, you can use matching thread and your stitching will look smoother.

4 **Fill a bobbin.** When practicing, use a bobbin thread that contrasts with the needle thread. This will allow you to check the tension in a later step.

5 **Thread the machine.** Put your thread on a thread stand if your machine doesn't have a built-in method to feed the thread off the top of the spool. Remember to release the needle tension while you are threading the machine; engage the tension right before you take the thread through the needle. Doing this insures that the thread is going through the tension disks properly.

Test stitching

Without worrying about what pattern is being created, do a little stitching to make sure everything is set up properly.

1 **Start the thread.** Hold the needle thread and take one stitch by turning the wheel slowly or, if your machine has the feature, tap the pedal. End with the needle in the up position. Pull on the needle thread; the bobbin thread should come to the top. Pull both the needle and bobbin threads beneath the free-motion foot and to the left of the needle to get them out of the way. You can use scissors, a seam ripper, or the thread itself to pull the needle thread down.

2 **Check the tension.** Make sure that the needle tension is engaged so you don't get a nest of thread on the back of the practice piece.

3 **Take a few small stitches to secure the thread.** Sew any small pattern. For example, sew an inch towards you, a little to the right, an inch away from you, a little to the right. To end, either cross over the starting threads, using small stitches, or end the line using small stitches.

4 **Release the needle tension; pull the work out of the machine.** Clip the bobbin thread a few inches away from the back of the work, leaving a few inches of thread still in the machine. Pull

up on the needle thread; this should pull a loop of bobbin thread to the top surface. Grab this loop with either your fingers, the point of your scissors, or a seam ripper, and pull the bobbin thread to the top. Examine the lines of stitching for even thread tension. Do you have "eyelashes" showing on the top? If so, the needle thread is pulling up the bobbin thread. Loosen the needle tension. If the eyelashes are on the bottom of the work, the bobbin tension is tighter than the needle thread. There are two ways to fix this. Tightening the needle tension is the easier method; however, I don't like to have the threads too tight, because it takes more effort on my part to move the quilt around when fighting the tension on the thread. I'd rather lower the bobbin tension. This is when having a second bobbin case comes in handy because a lot of people prefer not to play with the tension on their main case. Many sewing machine mechanics tell their customers never to play with the bobbin tension, but you can have your dealer show you how to adjust the bobbin case. One warning: if you have an embroidery machine, leave the bobbin case alone; bobbin tensions are set to tight tolerances necessary for embroidery.

5 **Check the pressure foot tension.** Were you able to move the felt easily under the needle? If the free-motion foot was pushing down on the quilt even when the needle was up, the pressure foot tension should be loosened if your machine has that option.

I like to think of my style of quilting as "organized meandering." I can't follow a pre-drawn line very well, so I make it up as I go. I don't like following directions, and I don't have a plan for what motif will go where before I start. When working on a full-sized quilt I start quilting in the center of the quilt and work towards the edge, shape by shape, concentrating on only the few inches surrounding the needle. I fill in a small area and then move on to the next. I do try to vary the motifs from shape to shape in the quilt. I might change the motifs from one based on straight lines to one based on curves; I may use spirals here, leaves there. It's more interesting to look at and more fun to quilt.

The motifs I will show you are presented in groups: rocking motifs, spirals, three-step motifs, braided motifs, and flowers. Practice the motifs in the order presented here. If one motif doesn't work for you, skip it and try another.

Here are some things to keep in mind as you practice the motifs:

1. I space my free-motion lines about ¼" apart. You can use the edge of the free-motion foot as a guide along previously sewn lines to help you space them. This distance might seem excessively close to some quilters—it takes about an hour to fill a square foot of a quilt this way. Feel free to quilt more loosely or tightly, whatever is comfortable to you.

2. Long straight lines are hard to keep straight; work in 1" lengths and then change directions. Long lines look nicer if they have a little bit of curve to them, so try putting a curve on a long line on purpose.

3. Don't look at the needle when you are quilting; look at the line you are drawing on the quilt. Just like you don't look at the lines on the side of the road, look ahead. When you are following the motifs in this book, do not look at the book while you are actually stitching. Keep your eyes on your work so you don't sew through your finger.

GET A GRIP

Many people think that they have to keep their hands perfectly flat against the machine bed and should move the quilt by pushing down on it. This is hard to do, especially for long periods of time. Some people wear gloves to get a better grip; others end up with achy hands after an hour of free-motion quilting.

You do not have to push down on the quilt to keep it flat on the sewing machine bed. The quilt does have to be kept flat, because if the quilt flaps up, you'll get skipped stitches. But, it is the job of the free-motion foot to hold the quilt down; your job is to move the quilt around in a smooth motion. This is much easier to do if you can grip the quilt in your fist. You may want both hands gripping from the top, or one hand on top and one under the quilt. I shift mine around.

To prove that your quilt doesn't have to be flat, try this: grab a practice square in your fist, and gently pull it up, forming an inverted cone. Run the machine, stitching in circles. See how the foot holds the quilt down?

robbi's ramblings...

" Don't worry about consistent stitch length. That will come with practice. Yes, judges occasionally comment that my stitch length varies, but I've won ribbons for my free-motion quilting anyway. My feeling is that varied-length stitches are a mark of a human being moving the quilt around, not a machine. Consider a pencil or pen drawing: the line thickness indicates the work was done by hand. Computer drafting programs will give perfectly smooth lines. Art is done by hand. We are doing art here. Strive for small enough stitches that the line will be smooth, but not so small that you can't pick out the stitches with a seam ripper. "

ROCKING MOTIFS

These motifs are created by "rocking" back and forth and are the simplest to learn. One thing to keep in mind is not to let the motifs grow too big; stop before the lines get too long and clumsy.

1 **Start practicing with the first motif.**

Motif A

At the corner, pause a second to let the machine complete the stitch. If you keep getting rounded corners try to make the corners square by pulling the work deliberately to the left with your left hand. Then pull the work down with your right hand.

If you can't make the corners square and you get rounded corners, that's OK. We'll call this Motif B.

Motif B

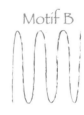 

Don't worry if some of your corners are square and some are round. It will get better as you practice. Remember that the overall appearance is what's important; when there is a lot of quilting, the rounded corners won't be so noticeable.

4 To train your brain, practice drawing a motif with a pen on paper before you stitch.

5 Your thread choices will affect how the quilting lines look. Thread that contrasts with the quilt fabric will highlight any imperfections. Matching thread will blend in. Variegated threads will distract the eye and entertain it with color changes. Practice with different combinations of thread to see which you like better.

6 Keep in mind that the viewer doesn't know the motif you were trying to achieve; they see only the results. If a motif isn't working for you, but something else emerges that you like, go with that.

7 Imperfect sections will be hidden in the abundance of quilting. The overall effect is what matters. Don't sweat what you perceive to be small errors.

8 I don't rip anything out unless there is a big problem, like bunching on the back of the quilt, a thread nest, or a thread that looks just plain ugly.

9 It's OK for the quilting lines to cross and/or touch each other. In fact, many of the motifs in this book rely on that.

10 This is supposed to be fun. Listen to music. Get comfy. Have everyone leave you alone.

2 **Make a line of Motif A.**

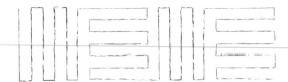

Adjust the spacing or add more lines to fill the square. The motifs don't have to be identical; just keep the "theme" going. I changed the color of the line to help you see the direction changes.

3 **Fill a square.** To fill a square, you can make a row of Motif A, and then come back from right to left.

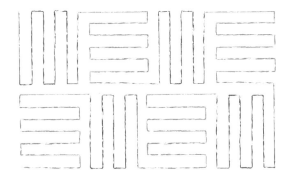

You can also do one motif and move down, then move to the right, and then up.

Again, you don't have to be perfectly consistent. Mix up sections of rows and sections of squares.

4 **Try doing Motif B (with rounded corners) in a line and in a square.**

5 **Here's a motif adapted from Japanese sashiko patterns.** Once you can do the motif, practice it in a line or in a square.

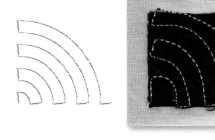

Right: Detail of "Still Life with Fruit" 17" x 23"

Different free-motion quilting motifs help to accent and distinguish each element in this quilt.

6 **This rocking motif looks like flower petals.**

The petal is started from the center, rocking up and over, back and forth. This one is started with a counterclockwise loop. You can start in either direction. If you add an even number of loops, it will end on the same side you started. With an odd number, you'll be on the other end. Don't go right back to the starting point on each swing, end a little higher on the curve each time.

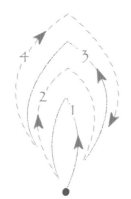

7 To continue adding petals, start a new one where you ended the first. After that, you can start a new petal in the "valleys" between two petals. In the diagram below, the second petal has three loops because it ends on the left, the third petal has four loops because it ends on the right. Both started with counterclock wise loops. Petals can also have different numbers of swings.

Try coming up with new patterns by varying the line as you rock back and forth, making points, curves, and so on.

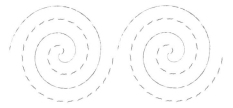

SPIRAL MOTIFS

1 **The simplest spiral is a round spiral.**

To make a spiral, sew in towards the center (solid line), leaving a "lane" with enough room to come back out again (dotted line). Spirals can start out clockwise or counterclockwise.

2 **Experiment with the many different spiral patterns.** For example, make the spirals in a row.

3 **Change directions and work back to fill space.** Nest the spirals a bit for a pleasing look.

You can also travel back to the beginning of the row by following the outline back.

Left: "Shoot the Moon" • 40" x 52"
Using contrasting colors of threads on a quilt can show off your free-motion quilting quite nicely.

4 Experiment with your spirals—they can be square, triangular, or leaf shaped.

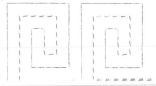

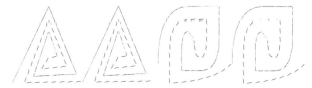

THREE-STEP MOTIFS

1 I call the following motifs "three-step" because you sew one step forward (1), one step back to where you came from (2), and then the third step forward again (3). After that, you keep going in the direction you want to fill.

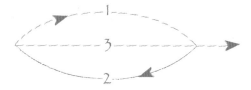

2 You can take a longer step back; in this motif, the second step was a spiral.

3 Narrow your motif a bit and make a leaf. Keep your motif going and make a row.

4 Finish one row and work your way back with another row nestled below.

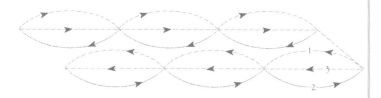

5 Angle the first leaf up, the next one down, and then make the third one going back. Keep doing this to fill up a space.

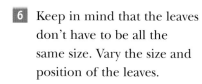

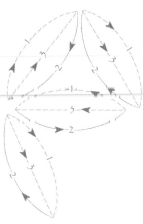

6 Keep in mind that the leaves don't have to be all the same size. Vary the size and position of the leaves.

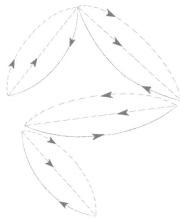

BRAIDED MOTIFS

Braided motifs are made up of S-shapes, moving up and down and then swirling around. Using pencil and paper to practice a bit may help you figure out the more complicated shapes. This is one motif group where I get in the mindset that I will aim at a motif, but if something else appears, I'll go with that.

1 Make S-shapes moving up and down and to the right. Here, the solid line is moving up, and the dashed line is moving down.

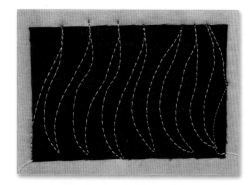

2 For this motif, start at the circle, move down, and then move to the left and up. Next, move down, around, and end at the lower right. Keep moving up and down, wrapping the lines to the left, but ending lower and to the right a bit. *(Figure A)*

3 When you get tired of going lower, or run out of room, start adding S's on the right side, moving up. This makes a leafy shape. *(Figure B)*

4 For this motif, add another row going down and to the right. You can keep adding more rows, up and down, working to the right. *(Figure C)*

5 When you get bored moving up and down, start a spiral and pile up S-shapes going around the spiral. Now you have a flower. *(Figure D)*

6 Leaves can be made by outlining the leaf shape and then filling in with S-shapes. *(Figure E)*

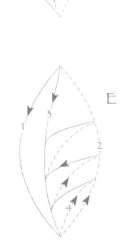

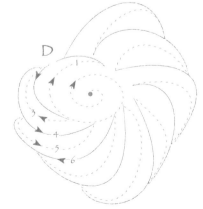

FLOWER MOTIFS

There are a few tricks when making flowers. You can start in the center of the first flower and work your way out. But how do you then get into the center of the next flower? You can either pick a center point a few inches away from where you ended the first flower, stitch along one edge of a "petal to be" and then work from there. Or, you can start making partial flowers, visualizing a bouquet or a flowerbed, where you wouldn't be able to see every single flower as a full flower.

Flowers are combinations of the motifs presented earlier; have fun inventing new flowers as you go along. Your flowers, just like nature, will have some variation.

1 Below, the flower on the left consists of pointy petals worked in a circle. Complete one full petal, then move to the next, but don't worry if you can't fit five identical petals around the center. Adjust the shape as necessary; your flower may have four or six petals. On the right is the same petal with rounded tips. Try mixing up the two petal shapes in a space.

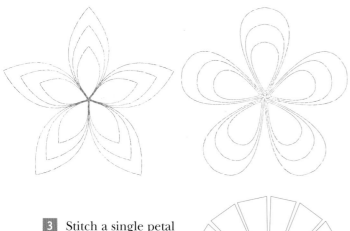

3 Stitch a single petal shape and then use it for the center of a flower. The petals of this flower are angular.

4 You can round off the petals or make the petals pointy.

5 Try making some flowers with spirals in the center.

COMBINING MOTIFS

If you have a larger area to fill, you can make it more interesting by combining two or more motifs. For example, I might start out with a curvilinear pattern, such as the petals, and move the motif along in one direction for a while, perhaps at an angle. Then I'll go back and fill in space around the petals with a motif that is more angular; when I get bored with that, I'll switch to another motif. The more motifs you use, the more interesting it will be for you to quilt it, and the more interesting it will be for the viewer to see it.

FINDING NEW SOURCES FOR MOTIFS

You may start seeing new quilting motifs whenever you see a strong linear design. Designs don't have to be continuous; with a little bit of playing, you can find a way to stitch designs together. It's OK to double back over a line of stitching or to travel between shapes. Keep in mind that longer, straight segments are harder to do gracefully than shorter, curvier segments. Books on ornamental metal or Mexican pottery will yield patterns you can modify easily.

QUILTING WITH VARIEGATED THREADS

Variegated threads add excitement to the surface, create a diversion for the viewer's eye, and make your quilting look smoother. Variegated threads come in rayon, polyester, and metallic. The color assortments vary, too; some are several shades of the same color, for example, light blue, medium blue, and dark blue. Other variegated threads are combinations of colors, for example, turquoise, fuchsia, and purple, all on one spool. These threads can be entertaining to watch as you stitch, too. Try the motifs shown earlier with variegated threads and see if your stitching doesn't look smoother already.

There are a few tricks you can do with variegated thread. First, try isolating a color with a single motif. Start stitching a motif, and when you see the thread color change, start a new motif right away or as soon as you can. Eventually, you'll have filled a space with leaves or whatever, with each one stitched in one color. Don't worry that it takes a while to get it going. No one will notice that you didn't get them all working right from the start; they'll just notice the cool overall mosaic effect.

Another approach is to play what I call "musical threads." I pick two motifs, let's say square spirals and round spirals. When the thread color changes, I change motifs. Often the color changes are fast enough that two colors have to be grouped in one motif. When the second color comes up, it's time to work my way out of the spiral.

FREE-MOTION QUILTING WITH PROGRAMMED STITCHING

So, you may have this expensive sewing machine with lots of fancy stitches and all I've told you to use is the simple straight stitch. Now we can play with some of the programmed stitches. Normally these stitches are used with the feed dogs down, letting the machine control the stitch length. However, if you set up the machine for free-motion quilting, the programmed stitches can be used, letting the machine control the sideways movement of the needle while you move the quilt back and forth.

Before playing with programmed stitching, make sure you have the regular stitch plate on the machine. If you leave the single stitch plate on, you'll break a needle before you start. Also, make sure the left and right swing of the needle fits within the opening of your free-motion foot, so you don't break the needle on the foot. You may have to adjust the stitch width to stay within the foot. This is an instance when having a wider free-motion foot is an advantage. Turn the machine manually through a few stitches to make sure your needle won't hit something and break.

Stitches that mostly go forward while moving sideways are an advantage here because they are smoother to work with. My favorite is a three-step zigzag. I think it's meant for applying elastic. Figure F shows how it looks when sewn normally using the feed dogs and a regular foot. Figure G shows how it looks when you free-motion with it.

Let the machine swing the needle sideways and stitch up and down. You can try to line up the curves, or let them run over each other. If you move the work swiftly to the left or right yourself, the machine will just make a straight horizontal line.

FREE-MOTION QUILTING WITH A TWIN NEEDLE

If one luscious thread is good, two are even better. Twin needles will give you two lines of quilting in the same time it takes for one. The needles come in various widths; try an assortment to see what you like. One proviso—you will get a zigzag line on the back of the quilt. Make sure you use your regular stitch plate with the twin needle, and verify that both needles fit in the opening of your free-motion foot. Check your machine manual to see how to thread it with two threads. Use thread stands if necessary to hold both spools.

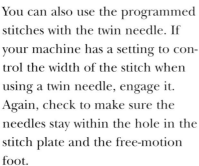

You can also use the programmed stitches with the twin needle. If your machine has a setting to control the width of the stitch when using a twin needle, engage it. Again, check to make sure the needles stay within the hole in the stitch plate and the free-motion foot.

Try using two different colors, or one solid and one variegated; add metallic threads into the mix. There are infinite possibilities.

FILLING IN BORDERS

When quilting a border, I start in the lower right corner, with the bulk of the quilt on the table instead of in my lap, and sew along the border as if I were driving along a narrow road.

Sometimes I like to have a wavy motif move along the border. To get some regularity, I mark a center wavy line around the border, and "bounce" motifs along that line. I can do petals all oriented upward and to the left, on the inside of the line, all the way around the quilt, then come back and work on the outside of the line. The finished border will resemble a feathered cable. You can work the second line of petals pointing down for another effect. Fill one side of the line with one motif, the other with another. Consider a change of color on each side of the line. Another variation is to mark circles along the border; quilt one design within the circles, and then fill outside the circles with another motif.

PREPARING THE QUILT

Batting

My preference is for a wool batting. Wool battings have a lot of loft that shows off the excessive free-motion quilting I put into a quilt. Since my quilts get pulled out of shape by the quilting process, a wool-batted quilt can simply be steam pressed to lay flat. A wool batting also has more body than polyester, which makes it easier to manipulate when free-motion quilting. Wool battings are somewhat translucent. This translucency helps when trimming the batting to the right size, because you can lay it down on top of the quilt top and see where to trim. Because I don't plan to wash my quilts, I don't pre-wash the batting.

Don't baste—fuse! I prefer to fuse my top and backing to my batting. I used to use whole sheets of fusible to baste, but in the last few years, I've found that I can simply use the scraps of fusible leftover from creating the quilt top.

Fusing the batting

1. If possible, work on a table that is larger than at least one dimension of your quilt. Don't use a good dining table. Cover the table with a layer of batting or felt to create a giant ironing board.

2. Using steam, iron the top one more time to make sure all the pieces are securely stuck to the background and there are no wrinkles. Flip the top over, and repeat.

3. Lay the batting over the back of the quilt top, smooth it out without stretching it, and trim it to be a few inches bigger than the quilt top on each side.

4. Fold half of the batting back to expose half of the back of the quilt top.

robbi's ramblings...

" Before you free motion quilt your 'real' quilt, practice your motifs again on a quilt square made up of your batting and fabric. Don't start on your real quilt until you feel warmed up and have the machine set up to your satisfaction. The tension should be good, the thread colors should look right, and your quilting should be smooth and graceful. Return to your practice square if your machine starts acting up; fix the problem using samples on your practice square, not the real quilt. You can throw out a practice square, but if the thread is nesting on the back of your real quilt, you have to rip stuff out. I try to practice for about half an hour before I start a quilt, but I get impatient after about 15 minutes and decide I'm warmed up. My quilting gets better after a few hours of quilting. Later, when I look at the first quilting, I often regret that I didn't practice more before starting. If you see one of my quilts in person, look at the stitching starting from the center out—the outer stitching will invariably be nicer. If it's not, it's likely I quilted more than one quilt in a row and you are looking at the second or third quilt. "

5. Take fusible scraps and peel them away from the paper. Lay them out on the quilt top a few inches apart. It is not necessary to cover the entire surface with a solid layer of fusible. If you run out of scraps, cut up some sheets of webbing into scraps.

6. Unfold the batting and lay it down on the top again, gently, so you don't dislodge the fusing scraps.

7. Steam iron on the batting, starting at the center and gently working towards the edges. Don't stretch anything. The iron shouldn't stick to the wool batting.

8. Fold the unfused backing over the fused side, and repeat steps 5 and 6.

9. Flip the whole assembly over, so you can see the top, and steam iron again. Gently smooth out any wrinkles. If you do get wrinkles, reach between the top and batting, pull the batting off, and smooth out the wrinkle.

10. Flip the assembly over again. Lay the backing fabric on top of the batting, wrong side down, so you are looking at the right side of the backing fabric.

11. Trim the backing fabric to cover the batting, leaving a few inches extra on each side, if you have enough fabric. It's OK to use a pieced batting, and the seams can be wherever you want.

12. Fold back the backing, exposing the batting, and sprinkle fusible scraps around on the batting just like you did before. Repeat for the other half.

13. Steam press the backing.

Now wasn't that easy? If your quilt is small, you may even skip the fusing step. Wool batting has some bite to it and will stick to the cotton fabric used in your quilt top and backing. I will skip basting on a quilt that is up to about 3' x 3'. If you do this, it's smart to allow extra batting and backing in case things shift. A safety pin in the center and at each corner to hold it isn't a bad idea either.

BATTING TIPS

- Batting can be pieced. Simply lay the pieces down, overlapping the edges about a quarter inch. Wool batting will squish down enough. The fusing used for the basting will hold it all together.

- Buy batting in queen size. Cut out the size you need for a smaller quilt.

- Having a few inches extra on the edge will also make your life easier when quilting to the very edge of the top.

A FEW FINAL TIPS ON FREE-MOTION QUILTING

- Work from the center or from the top. The quilt will shrink up a bit as you quilt it. If you work from the center to the outside, this shrinkage will be uniform and move out to the edges. Leaving a few extra inches of batting and backing is smart because you may need those by the time you get to the edges.

- It is not necessary to do any stabilizing stitching before you start.

- I work in a spiraling pattern. Work from the center towards the right, changing colors as you go. Working towards the right side of the quilt means you are pulling more and more of the quilt out from underneath the neck of the machine, instead of trying to jam more into the machine. By the time you have quilted from the center to the right, you can probably quilt well enough to flip it over and work from the center to the right again, upside down. You can also work from the top to the bottom. Just pick one direction and keep going in that direction.

- Don't skip areas because when you come back, you may find it's hard to avoid wrinkles.

- Don't roll the quilt; put the right edge under the needle and slide the quilt into the machine until you get to the center. Support the back and left side of the quilt on a table. Take a deep breath and grab the center of the quilt and start quilting. Work in a small area, concentrating on four inches at a time. Remember that this is the hardest part to quilt; you have more of the quilt stuffed into the machine than you will at any other time. Remember to grip the quilt comfortably, using your hands both above and below the quilt if that is more comfortable.

- Start with a motif that mostly moves up and down; this is easier than trying to jam more of the quilt into the machine as you go.

- As you move towards the edge of the quilt, be careful not to quilt the excess backing into the quilt. If you do, and all the sewn-down fabric is excess, you can cut the backing close to the stitching lines and tease it out of the quilting without having to rip out all that stitching.

CHAPTER 5

I Finished It My Way

Sneak Peek

In this chapter you'll learn about:

- **Squaring off the quilt**
- **Designing and making a fused binding**
- **Making a hanging sleeve**
- **Making a label**

After the quilting is completed, there are a few things that should be done before you declare it ready to show off on your wall or at a quilt show. I have some very quick and simple methods to share with you.

Squaring off the quilt

I like my quilts to hang flat, without hills and valleys on the surface and without wavy edges. Extensive free-motion quilting can distort the surface of the quilt. Some quilters I know use elaborate methods to force their quilts into flatness, for example, by wetting them, pulling them into shape, and letting them dry. I wonder if their quilts will just distort again if they ever get wet and aren't blocked. In my approach, instead of blocking, I use a steam iron for a little friendly persuasion to get the quilt flat.

DIRECTIONS ✋

1. Steam press the quilt as flat as possible. Just press down, don't "scrub" it.

2. Use a grid or T-square ruler to mark the proposed edges of the quilt with a chalk marker or pencil. Before you cut, check the edges to see if opposites are parallel and the corners are square. If you have a long tape measure, measure the diagonals—they should be the same.

3. Using a rotary cutter, ruler or grid, and a mat, trim the quilt to the desired dimensions. Use good shears if you don't have a rotary cutting set, taking long, neat strokes to trim the edge.

Left: "Half Past Midnight" • 2000 • 63" x 63"
This still life was created at half an hour past the beginning of the new millennium. The binding on this quilt was cut with a wavy rotary blade, using the same fabric as the outer border so that it blends in.

COOL TOOL One of my favorite tools for marking 90-degree corners is a piece of plastic grid used for a suspended ceiling. The grid is 2' x 4' and is readily available at home improvement centers. It works just like a giant rotary cutter ruler; you can run a rotary cutter along the edge of it, or you can simply use it as a great big ruler, mark the cutting line with a pencil, and cut with a pair of shears.

DESIGNING THE BINDING
FABRIC

If you don't want to see the binding, use the same fabric you used on the outer edge of the quilt, the background, or the border. However, a binding that contrasts with the outer edge of the quilt can make a visual frame. Using a fabric that has already made an appearance in the quilt again on the binding creates a nice effect. Sometimes I use a one-inch border between the central design of the quilt and an outer border. Another technique is to change the color of the binding as you move around the quilt.

robbi's ramblings...

" Traditionally, binding is used to enclose the edges of the quilt so that the batting doesn't leak out. There are many traditional ways to apply a binding to a quilt. Usually, long strips with turned edges are sewn to either the top or bottom surface of the quilt, the binding is turned over the edge, and then it is sewn down either by hand or machine.

I don't like to do it that way. I've tried using bias binding, crosswise-cut binding, lengthwise-cut binding—the direction of the strip doesn't seem to make a difference—no matter what I do. The binding seems to stretch the edges of the quilt and make it wave. For me, mitering the corners the traditional way is a big pain. I can't seem to sew the second edge down neatly by machine, and hand stitching makes my hands hurt. And it takes forever. In 1997, I started fusing my bindings on, holding them down with decorative stitching, and I've never gone back to regular sewn bindings.

When I show my technique to students, they are often surprised that "The Judges" will accept a fused binding. Not only will they accept it, every quilt of mine that has won a ribbon has had a fused binding. In the beginning, I often received comments on my "innovative" binding method. The Judges also critiqued the workmanship of my fused bindings, so if you are worried about what The Judges think, make sure your craftsmanship is excellent. "

HOT HINT When cutting binding strips with a shaped rotary blade, practice with an old ruler to learn how to cut without nicking your good ruler. I've found if I concentrate on pressing down on the cutter, instead of pressing forward, I can cut a nice edge without ruining my ruler. Also, you want to press down with confidence because skips in the cut shaped edge are harder to repair than in a straight edge. To fix a skip, line up the blade with the pattern already cut and press down. Or even easier, plan to cut a few extra strips and don't worry about the skips. You don't have to use a full strip every time; you can cut out any bad parts and fuse.

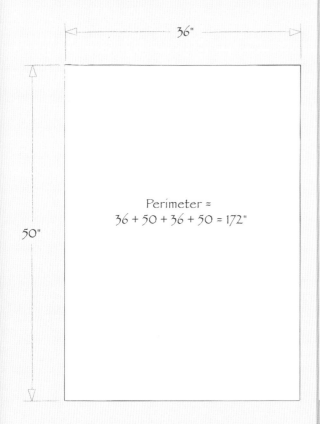

Perimeter =
36 + 50 + 36 + 50 = 172"

Opposite: "Shuffle" • 2002 • 18" x 18" • This quilt was bound using different colors of fused binding strips. The orange and yellow strips were ironed on first, and then the blue strips in the corners were ironed on, overlapping the yellow and orange. Doing the binding in short sections allowed me to contrast it with the adjacent blocks.

SHAPE

What shape? We'll be cutting the binding strips with a rotary cutter, but you needn't be limited to a straight edge. Rotary blades are available with pinked edges, wavy edges, scalloped edges, and deckled edges. Some manufacturers don't recommend certain blades for use with fabric, but the truth is that because we are putting fusible webbing on the fabric before cutting, you can use any blade that will give you a clean cut.

The shape of the binding edge should complement the design of the quilt. A whimsical quilt with bold colors will love having a wavy-edged binding. A more formal design may call for a straight edge. The only warning I have on using a straight-edged binding is that it has to be perfectly straight or The Judges will notice any deviation. A shaped edge can be a little wonky without drawing as much attention.

MAKING THE BINDING

DIRECTIONS ✋

1. Measure the perimeter of the quilt. Let's assume you want to bind a 36" x 50" quilt. The perimeter is 172" (36 + 50 + 36 + 50).

2. To figure out how many strips of binding fabric you will need, first measure the usable width of the fabric. Assuming that your binding fabric has a useable width of 40", divide the quilt perimeter by 40 to find out how many strips you will need (172 ÷ 40 = 4.3). Round up your number of strips (4.3 to 5), and add one extra for safety to give you the total number of strips to cut (6). In this example, we will allow for 1" wide strips.
(***Note:*** *If you use decorative rotary cutter blades to cut the strips, allow for a few extra strips to compensate for any cutting errors. Test a strip on one of your practice squares to determine the width to cut the strips.*)

Determining the width of your binding strips
The edges of the binding strips won't be turned under as in a traditional sewn binding. To figure the width to cut the binding strips, decide how wide your finished binding will be, double this measurement, and add $\frac{1}{8}$" to allow for the thickness of the quilt. Generally I use a strip that is $\frac{3}{4}$" or 1" wide.

Making a fused binding

robbi's ramblings...

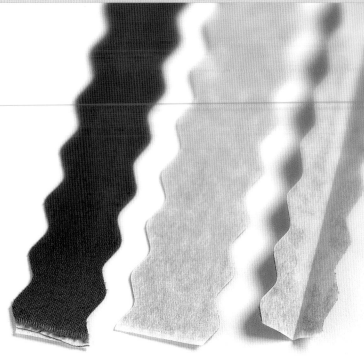

3 When you cut the binding strips, add a few extra inches to the length to make it easier to cut the strips straight. In our example, we add an extra 2" to the 6" strips for a total length of 8". Rotary cut an 8" piece across the width to create an 8" x 40" piece of binding fabric.

4 Using fusible webbing that is 18" wide, cut a 21" length piece of fusible webbing. Turn this piece, which is 18" x 21", sideways. Cut two 8" x 21" long strips from this piece. Iron the fusible webbing onto the binding fabric, overlapping where necessary to completely cover the binding fabric.

5 Leaving the paper on the webbing, trim the edges evenly. Then rotary cut 1" strips across the width of the prepared fabric. You'll probably end up with 7 strips. That's fine. Extra is good.

6 Fold each strip the long way, with the paper-backed sides together. Steam press. This crease line will help you apply the binding evenly along the edge of the quilt. Trim off the ends where there is no fusible webbing.

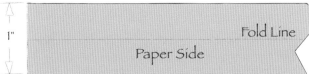

1" | Paper Side | Fold Line

.5" | Fabric Side
Fold Line

7 Peel the paper off the binding strips. The fold line will stay, giving you a centerline to apply the binding evenly.

8 Lay the quilt down on the ironing surface, top side down. You are now looking at the back of the quilt.

Carefully iron along edge of back of quilt

Binding under quilt top

Wrong side of binding

10 Iron the back of the quilt along the bottom edge to adhere the binding to the front of the quilt. Don't iron over the half of the binding that extends beyond the quilt, or webbing will get all over the iron. When the binding reaches the corner of the quilt, only iron to the corner of the quilt and stop.

11 The half of the binding strip that will be folded over to cover the back is now warm enough that it will stick. Carefully fold it over and finger press it down on the back of the quilt.

12 Steam iron down this section of the binding. Stop pressing when you get to the corner.

9 Starting at least 6" from the lower right corner, moving left, lay the binding strip down on the ironing surface, fusible side up. Line up the ironed centerline with the edge of the quilt.

Back of Quilt

Center line of binding

Fused side of binding

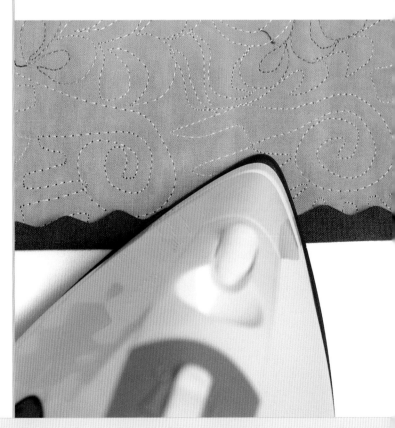

Making a fused binding

Wrong side of binding

Bindings under quilt top

13 When you reach a corner, stick your thumb inside the free end of the binding. Fold a miter in the corner, line up the fold with the edge of the quilt, and iron this new edge. It's often easier to iron down the binding on the new edge of the quilt for a few inches, then go back and fuss with the miter.

Right side of binding

← Binding going on clockwise around quilt.

14 Add strips by overlapping the new strip ¼" over the old on the front. Tack it quickly with the iron, and keep going. If using a decorative edge, match the motifs on the front, and don't worry about the back.

15 When you come back to where you started, overlap the end ¼" over the end of the first strip.

16 Go back over the whole binding to make sure it's ironed down very well.

Now that your binding is ironed down, it will need to be stitched to hold it in place permanently. Before this step, make a hanging sleeve and pin it to the back of the quilt so you can attach the sleeve at the same time you sew on the binding.

Right: "Vessels IV: Blown Glass" • 1998 • 72" x 54" • This quilt was designed by tracing outlines of various vessels from magazines and then putting the shapes together. The design was done in two layers. In the first layer, there is a set of vessels standing side by side on a table without overlapping. The second layer was made by overlaying the floating objects over the first layer. Before quilting the outer border, I drew a wavy line down the center of each border and used that as a guide line to quilt the large scallops. The binding on this quilt is out of the same fabric as the outer border, and it was cut with a wavy blade rotary cutter.

Making a hanging sleeve

MAKING THE SLEEVE

1 Cut or rip a piece of fabric that is the same width as your quilt and 24" long.

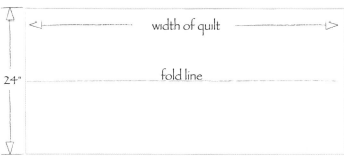

24"

width of quilt

fold line

2 With right sides together, fold the piece the long way. The piece is now the width of your quilt and 12" long on each side.

two raw edges

12"

width of quilt

folded edge

These directions are for making a 5" deep sleeve. The outer (or back) edge of the sleeve is 6" deep. Because the outer edge of the sleeve is bigger, it makes a nice D-shaped pocket for the hanging rod to rest in. The D-shape is created by folding the sleeve fabric and topstitching the top and bottom edges to make the fold permanent. Your quilt won't be deformed by the hanging rod poking out the front. The sleeve is double thickness, which means that you'll have two layers of fabric between the rod and the back of your quilt, which will protect your quilt from damage from a rough rod or dirt. I make a 5" sleeve even though most shows ask for a 4" deep sleeve. The extra inch makes it easier to slide the quilt onto the rod; the sleeve won't be so tight that the quilt puckers. For the sleeve fabric, I use leftover material from the quilt backing if I have it, so that the sleeve blends in; otherwise, any piece of cotton fabric will work, even plain muslin.

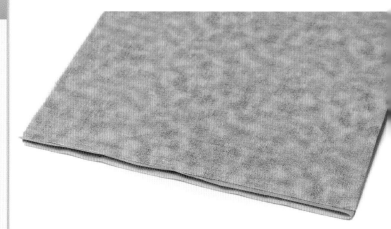

3 Sew ½" from each 12" edge. Then turn right sides out and press. The other way to do it is to fold wrong sides together and serge the edges, cutting off ½" on each side.

12"

sew here

sew here

folded edge

4 You now have a double thickness piece that is the width of the quilt and 12" long. Treat this as a single layer now. Fold the top and bottom edges together and press. Open the piece. This pressed line is a centerline for the next step.

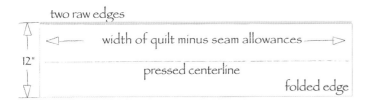

two raw edges

← width of quilt minus seam allowances →

12"

pressed centerline

folded edge

5 Fold the top edge (which has the two raw edges) down to the centerline. Fold the bottom edge (which is a folded edge) up to the centerline.

6 Topstitch along the top and bottom edges.

6"

7 Sew together the edges that are now in the center using a ½" seam allowance.

5"

Left: A side view of the sleeve after step 7. The top, curved side is the "good" side of the sleeve. The bottom, flat side goes against the quilt.

Below: View of the back of the sleeve

6"

Finishing the sleeve

1 Lay the side of the sleeve with the seam against the back of your quilt, lining up the top of the sleeve with the top of your quilt. Center the sleeve between the side edges of the quilt.

2 Decoratively stitch around the quilt twice, along the edges of the binding. This will attach the top edge of the sleeve to the quilt.

3 Hand stitch along the bottom edge of the sleeve to attach that edge to the back of the quilt.

4 Hand stitch the sleeve to the quilt along the vertical edges to keep someone from inadvertently sliding a pole between the sleeve and your quilt.

MAKING YOUR LABEL

5 Sew or fuse a label to the lower right corner of your quilt. I like to take a hunk of fabric, put fusible webbing on the back, cut it out, and then with a permanent pen write the title of the quilt, the copyright mark with the year and my name (©2004 Robbi Joy Eklow), address, phone number, and when I remember, the size of the quilt. I then fuse it to the back of the quilt. If you have a guitar you made as a sample, it makes a cute label.

HOT HINT Decorative stitches: If your machine has decorative stitches, look for one that would complement the shape of the binding if you used a shaped edge. Some machines have stitches that will reproduce the shape of the cut edge. Don't bother trying to line up the motifs in the stitching with the motifs in the binding. Just sew around the binding willy-nilly, keeping the edge of the quilt lined up straight with either the edge of your presser foot or a mark on the machine bed. Stop at each corner and rotate the quilt.

Right: "Prince of Cups" • 2000 • 40" x 52" • The top for this puzzle quilt was created in one day—the only time I've done that for a large quilt. I traced the edges of all the objects onto tracing paper and then moved the cut-out pieces around to get the composition. There is a layer of muslin holding the whole quilt together. The central image was fused onto the muslin, and then the outer border was fused onto the muslin, cutting the miters out of the border. A 1" border was fused on top of the edge where the central image and the wide border meet. This 1" border covers the raw edges and acts as a "mat" for the "frame" of the outer border. The binding was then created with fused strips of the same fabric as the 1" border, using a regular rotary blade.

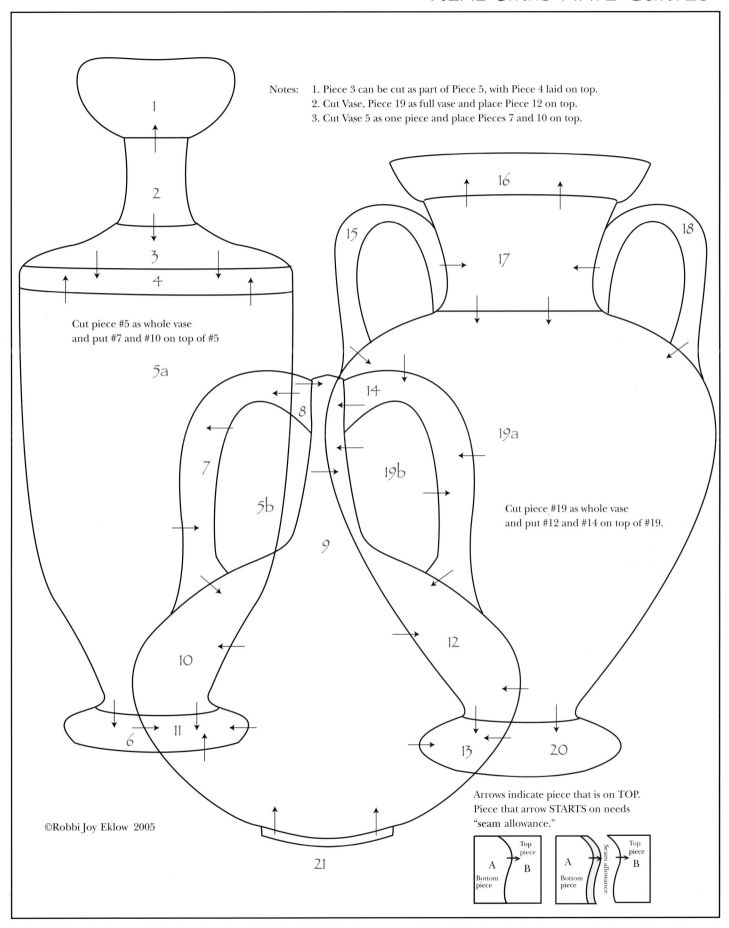

Notes: 1. Piece 3 can be cut as part of Piece 5, with Piece 4 laid on top.
2. Cut Vase, Piece 19 as full vase and place Piece 12 on top.
3. Cut Vase 5 as one piece and place Pieces 7 and 10 on top.

Cut piece #5 as whole vase
and put #7 and #10 on top of #5

Cut piece #19 as whole vase
and put #12 and #14 on top of #19.

Arrows indicate piece that is on TOP.
Piece that arrow STARTS on needs
"seam allowance."

©Robbi Joy Eklow 2005

GUITAR TRIO

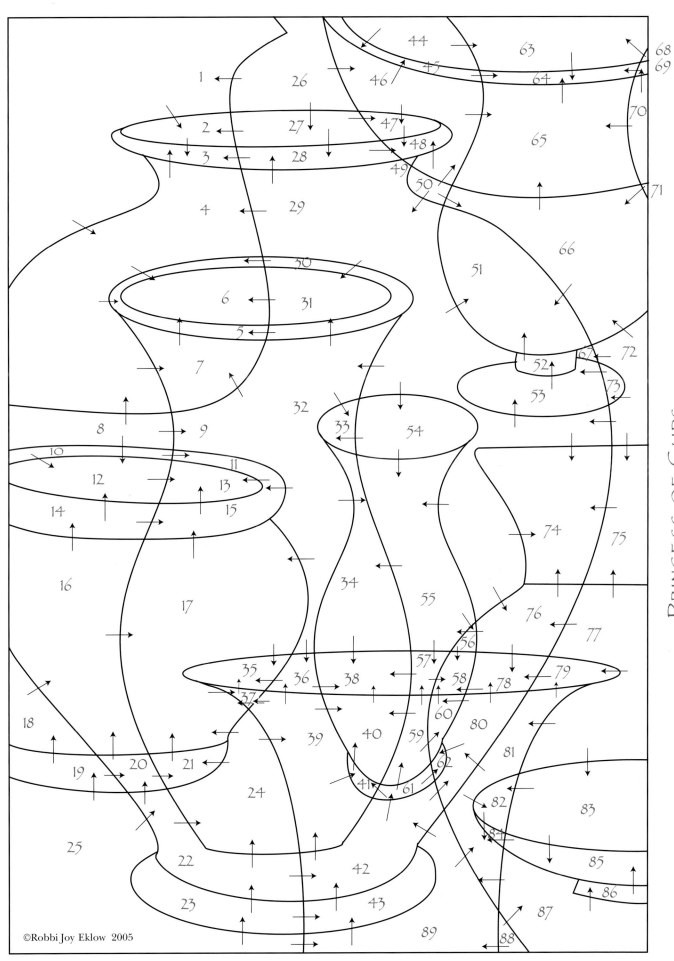

©Robbi Joy Eklow 2005

Free Expression: the Art and Confessions of a Contemporary Quilter

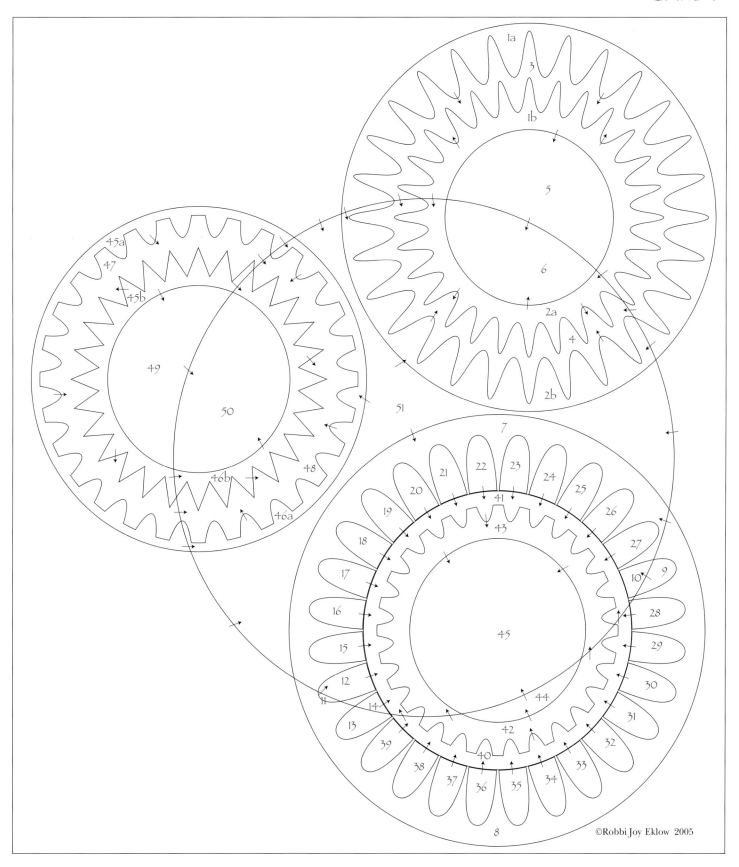

©Robbi Joy Eklow 2005

Free Expression: the Art and Confessions of a Contemporary Quilter

©Robbi Joy Eklow 2005

©Robbi Joy Eklow 2005

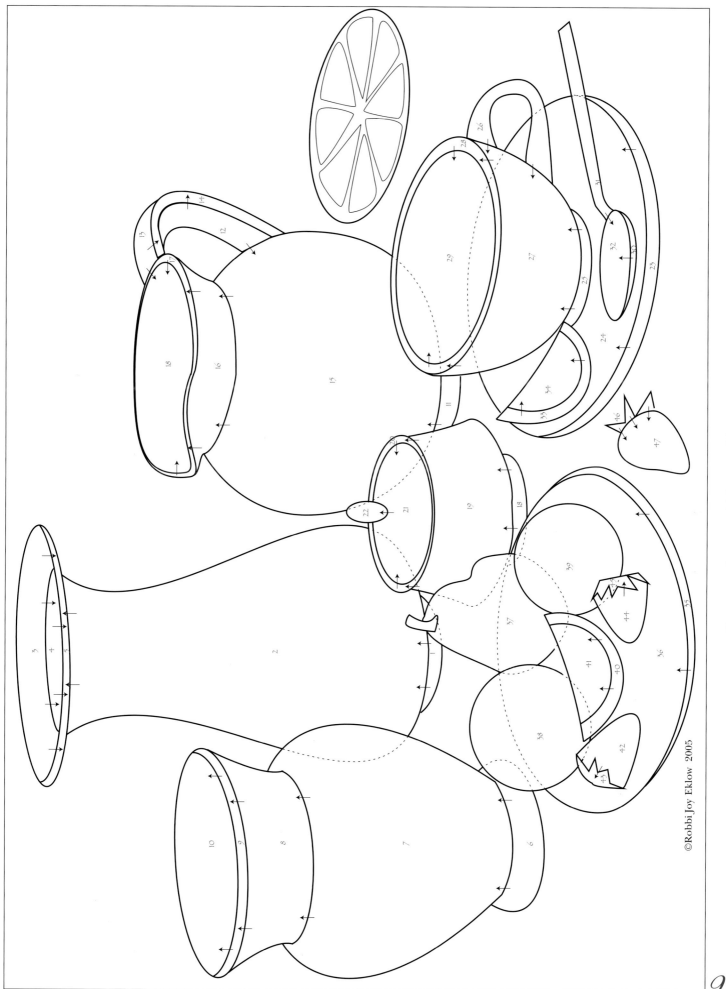

STILL LIFE WITH FRUIT

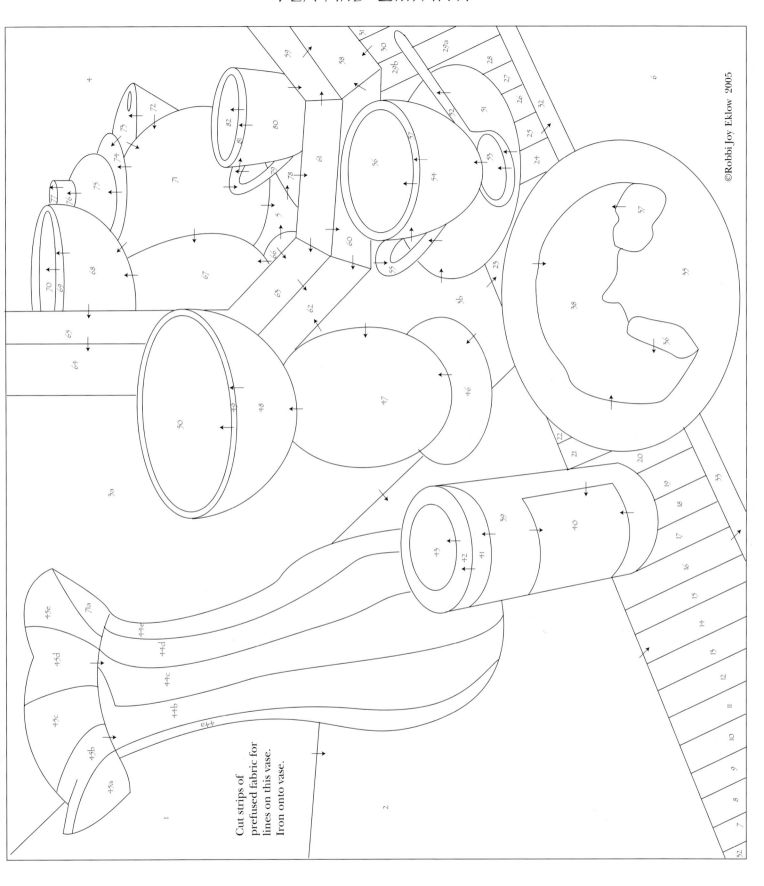

Cut strips of
prefused fabric for
lines on this vase.
Iron onto vase.

Dyeing to Get Started

Above: "Tea and Empathy" • 2000 • 60" x 64" • In this piece, I was able to use bigger pieces of hand-dyed fabric in the background. Note the fabric used in the lower left to imitate a wood table, and the fabric on the center right, used for a tablecloth. The fabric for the dish with the bagel was made by scrunching up fabric and letting the dye sit. The rest of the fabrics were all pour dyed.

WHY I DYE

I prefer to use hand-dyed fabrics in my quilts because I like the painterly effect they impart to the designs. Using my own fabrics gives me ownership of the entire quilt: I've dyed the fabrics, created the design, and machine quilted it myself. Another nice thing about dyeing fabric is that once you have made the initial purchase of dyes and cloth, all it takes is your time. If you need a medium purple with some red in it, you can create some. If you want a border that looks like a wood frame, you can dye a few yards instead of having to dash to the store and search for it. When you dye your own fabric, every piece looks different and sections of each fabric look different; your fabric is unique, and nothing is repeated. Of course, you don't have to use hand-dyed fabric in your quilts. My students usually bring in commercial prints, batiks, and hand dyes they have bought, and I have to admit that the palette available commercially is growing quickly. As for me, I'll still be dyeing my own fabrics for a long time—it's too much fun to stop and go shopping.

This chapter will give you the information you need to dye fabric using my techniques. Mine are just a few of an infinite number of ways to dye fabric. If you want to learn more about various dye techniques, see the resources listed in the bibliography. For beginners, this book can get you started; for experienced dyers, read on to compare notes, and maybe you will pick up a new technique.

After the fabric is soaked in a warm water/soda ash bath, I drape the fabric over a PVC pipe. Here I am pouring fuchsia dye onto the fabric in four places.

LEARNING TO DYE

My first suggestion to you is to get over the notion that you can make mistakes when dyeing. In my opinion, there is no "bad" dyed fabric. If I am aiming for deep purple and I end up with lilac, well, that's good—I'll have lilac to contrast with the deep purple. Or I could over-dye it with more purple and get a more interesting fabric than if I had just dyed deep purple from the start. I've learned that mixing specific colors is difficult, and even when I am successful, the process takes a few days. When I am in quilt-making mode, I am often tempted to dye some yardage that would just be perfect to fill an immediate need. But I rarely bother to stop during quilt-making and switch over to dyeing. I usually decide I'd rather keep quilting, and make a note to myself for my next dye session.

My second suggestion is to go with whatever "flow" you find yourself in on a dye day. When I am in dye mode, I dye whatever colors tickle my fancy that day. I might be trying for a nice yellow, end up with orange, and then decide the orange is really cool. Maybe some red would be nice with that, I think. I keep going until I run out of mixed dye, time, raw fabric (horrors), or until my attention span has been exceeded. Some days I dye 40 yards, some days four. And then there are those days I go down to the basement and clean up from my last session and lose steam just doing that.

The technique I use is a variation on pour dyeing, which is a direct application of dye rather than using a dye bath. Most of the fabrics in my quilts are dyed by hanging them up on a pole and pouring the dye down the yardage. With this "river of color," I use many different colors at once, letting the color mix right on the fabric and flow down.

robbi's ramblings...

" All dyed fabric is 'good.'

I had one dyed piece that came out half white because I hadn't used enough dye, and the colors didn't meet each other. I set it aside in my fabric stack to be over-dyed at another time. Later, when I was making my quilt 'Half Past Midnight,' I needed fabric for the wine glasses. This fabric was perfect when I cut around the white spaces. So, keep your fabric mistakes around for a while, and see if you can use them anyway. If you can't use them on the front, there's always yardage needed for the back of a quilt. "

My technique is very simple, and since I am not interested in being able to control or repeat the results, this is the best method for me.

All you need is the fabric, dye, hot water to provide heat for the chemical reaction, soda ash to provide alkalinity to force the molecules to combine, and some inexpensive equipment to mix, pour, and collect the runoff dye. Here are the basic steps that I will explain in this chapter:

1. Mix the dye.
2. Soak the fabric in soda ash and water.
3. Hang the fabric up.
4. Pour the dye down.
5. Let your creation "batch" so the dye can do its magic.
6. Wash out the excess dye.
7. Dry the fabric.
8. Iron it.
9. Admire it.

SHOPPING LIST

Fabric

I use good quality 100% cotton, bleached, mercerized PFD (prepared-for-dye) fabric. Fiber-reactive dyes will not work on polyester. Unbleached fabrics have a beige tint that will affect the final color, so for clearer colors, start with bleached fabric. Mercerization is a process that opens up the fibers to take more dye, resulting in colors that are about 25% darker than unmercerized fabric. PFD has no treatment such as for permanent press, and no sizing has been applied; these treatments can act as a resist, keeping the dye from interacting with the cotton. When you buy PFD fabrics, find out if you need to scour the fabric first. To scour fabric, wash it in hot water and Synthrapol to remove any impurities before dyeing. I prefer fabric that is truly PFD—ready to be dyed right off the bolt.

Here are some sources for good fabrics, along with descriptions based on information in their catalogs.

PRO Chemical & Dye   800.228.9393

- Cotton sheeting, style 100
  Bleached, mercerized muslin 78 x 76
  thread count; 44"– 45" wide

Dharma Trading   800.542.5227

- Mercerized cotton print cloth (CPC and MUS4)
  Bleached, mercerized, 80 x 80 thread count; 45" wide

- Kona cotton PFD
  Bleached, 60 x 60 thread count;
  45" wide.

Lunn Fabrics   800.880.1738

- Bleached dyers' cloth
  Bleached, mercerized 75 x 75 thread count; 42" wide

Dye

I use fiber-reactive dyes, which are synthetic chemicals that bond to the molecules of cotton in the fabric. The color goes into the fabric and stays there, which makes it light and colorfast. The hand of the fabric stays the same, as opposed to paints that sit on top of the fabric, making it stiffer and likely to rub off. Dyes come in 2 oz., 8 oz., and larger jars. The dyes do degrade over time but will keep a long time in powder form. To track how long it takes me to use up each color, I write the date I opened the dye on the lid of each jar. When I empty a jar, I throw the lid in a paper bag so that I know what colors to restock next time I order dyes.

Procion MX Fiber-Reactive Powder Dyes come in hundreds of colors. "Manufactured colors" are created to make one specific color. These are also referred to as homogeneous or self-shades. These colors have an "MX" designation, which means that every molecule in an MX turquoise will dye the fabric turquoise. If you buy an MX orange, for example, MX-2R, you will only see orange bits of dye—no yellow, no red, just orange.

Dye suppliers mix their own blends from the manufactured colors. An orange without an MX designation will be blended from some yellow dye, some red, and maybe a touch of some other color. Dyes with the same MX designation, for example MX-2R, will have different names from different manufacturers. Dharma calls it PR6 Deep Orange, while PRO Chemical & Dye calls it 202 PRO Strong Orange. Because Dharma Trading and Pro Chemical use different dye suppliers, there is no guarantee that the colors with the same MX code will be exactly the same.

AUXILIARIES

Soda ash

This dye fixative is necessary to raise the pH of the liquid to about 12, which causes the dye to react with the cotton. If you don't use soda ash, your dye will wash down the drain. You can buy Arm & Hammer washing soda at the grocery store, but buy the kind that doesn't have bleach. PH PLUS is pure soda ash packaged for swimming pools and is available at pool supply stores and discount stores. It comes in 5-pound containers, but if you want a lifetime supply, buy a 50-pound bag at a pool supply store. I keep my soda ash in plastic-bag lined buckets in my basement, because the paper bag it comes in could turn my whole basement into a soapy mess in a flood. You can also buy dye fixative, which is soda ash, from dye suppliers. Baking soda is not soda ash, and won't work.

MX Name	Dharma Trading	PRO Chemical & Dye
MX-8G	**PR1 Lemon Yellow**	108 PRO Sun Yellow
MX-GR	**PR3 Golden Yellow**	112 PRO Tangerine
MX-3R	PR4 Deep Yellow	104 PRO Golden Yellow
MX-2R	**PR6 Deep Orange**	202 PRO Strong Orange
MX-BRA	**PR9 Scarlet***	300 PRO Scarlet
MX-GBA	PR10A Chinese Red	
MX-5B	PR12 Light Red	305 PRO Mixing Red
MX-8B	**PR13 Fuchsia Red**	308 PRO Fuchsia
MX-2G	PR22 Cobalt Blue*	402c Mixing Blue
MX-G	**PR23 Cerulean Blue***	406 PRO Intense Blue
MX-4GD		414 Deep Navy
MX-G	**PR25 Turquoise***	410 PRO Turquoise
MX-R	PR26 Sky Blue	400 Basic Blue
MX-G	**PR117 Grape**	
MX-GN		801 Grape
MX-BR		802 Boysenberry

Above: MX colors available in 2005. Colors in bold are ones I recommend you start with. When mixing, some dyes need double the amount of powder, ask your supplier for information.

pH test paper

This paper comes in little rolls for about $10 and is available from dye suppliers. A little goes a long way. You tear off a 1" strip and dip it into the soda ash/water mixture to check the pH levels. You are aiming for a pH around 11 or 12. I use it all the time, because the standard amounts of soda ash given in dye books are more than I find I need to get the proper pH. Also, during the process, I add more hot water to my soda soak bucket, then more soda ash; using the test paper insures I've added enough.

Synthrapol

Synthrapol, available from dye suppliers, is used to help release the loose dye molecules and keep them from falling back on your fabric when you are rinsing it. You may also need it if you are going to scour your fabrics. Different manufacturers recommend different amounts, ranging from 1 tablespoon to $\frac{1}{4}$ cup per load, so be sure to check the label. In a pinch, use clear dishwashing liquid.

CHOOSING A WORKSPACE

I dye in the basement because that's where I can hang up the fabric and have easy access to the hot water and washing machine. And I can make a mess down there. If you don't have a basement, consider your garage, your back yard, or your driveway. You need access to about three gallons of very hot water (to soak the fabric in prior to dyeing), warm water (body temperature, to mix the dye concentrate), a place to hang up the fabric (perhaps a clothesline in the back yard, a broomstick suspended between two tables or chairs, or a rod hung from the garage ceiling), and a way to collect the runoff dye. The first time I used this method, I hung a broomstick between the two side metal pieces on a ladder and used a wallpaper tray to collect the water.

- Consider the environment when you are working; for example, I don't use our driveway because it drains into a storm sewer that runs into a small lake.

- The process is messy, so plan ahead about how to avoid getting dye splashed on your carpet when you carry fabric inside. Make sure the dyed fabric is safely wrapped in plastic, or wait until it is dry, to avoid drips.

- If you must work in your kitchen, cover your counters and remember not to use dye utensils for cooking. Clean up dye powder immediately.

- Don't leave plastic sheeting on your lawn for an extended time. I did that once and it took all summer to fix the dead patches created by the heat generated under the plastic from the sun. You might want to test a small patch to make sure the soda ash doesn't kill your grass, although friends who have dyed on their lawns tell me this isn't a problem.

Urea

Urea comes in granules and is available from dye suppliers or a feed or garden store. It makes the water "wetter" by breaking the surface tension. I got a lifetime supply for about $7. Some people swear by it; I can't really tell the difference, but I have it, so I'm using it. I keep some of it in a smaller container that I can lift up to my worktable and easily spoon out small amounts.

Salt

Salt is necessary when you are using dye baths with a lot of water. Pour dyeing, the technique in this book, is a direct application of dye, so I don't use salt.

Safety equipment

Ask the dye supplier what breathing apparatus and safety precautions they recommend for their products and follow their instructions. I wear a dust mask and gloves during dye mixing. I have two kinds of gloves: dishwashing gloves and latex gloves. Dishwashing gloves are of thick rubber and can be found with a lip around the edge of the cuff to keep dye from dripping down your arms. Latex gloves (available at drug stores) are better for mixing dye, as the rubber gloves are unwieldy. Wear safety goggles or glasses to protect your eyes from dye mishaps and to keep the soda ash, which is caustic, out of your eyes. Of course, keep your dye away from food and don't reuse utensils from your dye area with food.

EQUIPMENT FOR DYE CONCENTRATE MIXING

I make up all of the dye concentrates for one dye session before I begin. I pour one cup of plain water into a beaker, dump in the dye powder, stir it with a stick mixer, and pour it through a funnel into a plastic water bottle with a "sports cap." The measuring spoon, beaker, and funnel need to be rinsed between major color changes so you don't contaminate the colors. However, I arrange my dyes in color order: yellow, orange, red, purple, blue, green, then brown and black. I rinse my equipment only after the red, after the purple, and after the green. It's OK with me if a teensy bit of lemon yellow gets mixed into the golden yellow. And the golden yellow won't hurt the orange, but I don't want any yellow in a purple dye concentrate, because that will dull it. (When you have all three primary colors present, you get brown). Remember, I'm not worried about repeating my results; if I were, I'd probably stop and wash everything between colors. If you have multiples of the spoons, beakers, and funnels, you can go down the line and mix all your colors at once.

Half-gallon water container with a big opening

I fill this with hot water, take it to my worktable, and dip the measuring cup into it to get the one cup of water to mix with the dye powder to make the solution.

Thermometer

It's helpful to make sure your water for the dye solution is at about 95 degrees Fahrenheit. You can use your wrist to measure for body temperature, but it's hard when you are wearing gloves. You can use an aquarium thermometer, a metal thermometer, or a candy thermometer.

Measuring cups

Plastic cups work well, but keep them out of your kitchen after they are used for dye. I marked the one-cup line with a dark permanent marker to make it easier to see.

Beakers

These are good containers for mixing up the dye concentrate. I have about ten 1000 ml plastic beakers so I can keep mixing new colors without having to stop and rinse the containers. PRO Chemical & Dye carries nice ones that are inexpensive. You could also use large plastic cups, but the beakers are more stable to avoid spillage.

Measuring spoons

The measuring spoons get messy, so if you can find cheap ones, get several and you won't have to clean up as much. If you are using urea, make sure you have one tablespoon set aside just for that.

Battery-operated drink mixer

This little gadget runs on two AA batteries and comes with two attachments: a teeny whisk and a stick. My whisk fell apart after about five minutes, but the stick has lasted for years. The stick has a slit down the center and the "wings" fly out when you turn the mixer on. It works wonderfully to mix the dye powder into the water. This little gadget has saved me from spending hours of time trying to get the dye powder to dissolve. One hint: Never turn on the mixer unless it's immersed in the water.

Disposable plastic spoons

If you don't have the drink mixer, use plastic spoons to stir and to break up glops of dye.

Squirt bottles

I save empty water bottles that come with "sports tops," and I remove the labels. I also use them to dump water on things. If you use just one brand, it's easier to find the caps to match the bottles if you have them stored in a bucket. You will need one bottle for each dye color, four extra for a gradation piece, and one to use with soda ash and water later.

Waterproof permanent marker

Before you get the squirt bottles wet, label each with the name of the dye. After you mix the dyes, it's sometimes hard to tell the colors apart. I also mark bottles with blends I've made up in case I want to try them again.

Funnels

These help you pour the water into the squirt bottles. Bigger is better, as long as it fits in the top of the bottle. Little ones get clogged faster.

Paper towels

Fabric dyeing is messy so keep a roll of towels nearby. Old cloth towels also work well to wipe up spills.

Plastic sheeting

Use sheeting to protect the work surface.

Five-gallon bucket

This holds the soda ash/water solution and eight yards of fabric to soak before dyeing. I put a short length of hose, leftover from my old washing machine, on my basement sink faucet. With this, I can leave the bucket on the floor instead of lifting it in and out of the sink.

Mixing stick

Use a big stick or dowel to stir up the soda ash in the water bucket without having to get your hands in there. It is also helpful for poking the fabric down into the bucket.

Hanging pole and drip catcher

For a hanging pole, I use a 10' long piece of electrical conduit, bought at a home improvement store for $1. It hangs horizontally from the beam in my

After I pour the first color onto the fabric in four places, I add the second color. Here I am pouring yellow dye onto the fabric in four places adjacent to the fuchsia stripes.

basement, about 6½' above the floor. I place plastic snow sleds underneath to catch the drips, and protect the floor under that. The 10' long pole allows me to dye more than one piece in a session and leave the fabric hanging to dry. You could use a broomstick or dowel supported between two tables, with a plastic storage bin beneath to catch drips. Wallpaper wetting trays will also work, but you have to be more careful to line up the fabric right over the tray. You will get a line from selvedge to selvedge across the fabric where it rested on the pole. Keep that in mind if you want long pieces with no interruptions.

MIXING THE DYE CONCENTRATE

1. Put down a row of paper towels towards the back of your workspace.

2. On the paper towels, lay out a row of dye powders in color order from left to right: light yellow, darker yellow, orange, red, fuchsia, purple, turquoise, dark blue, dark green, light green, and so on.

3. Mark the lid of each dye jar with the color number, the color name, and the date you opened the jar. Some dyes need double or more powder to give full strength; the supplier will indicate that (for example, turquoise or

any color mixed from turquoise). If this is the case, mark it right on the lid. Pull the sealing tape off the lid, but don't open the jars yet.

4. Before you get the bottles wet, take one squirt bottle and use a permanent marker to label it with the first color name and number. Place it behind the matching dye jar. Go down the line and do this for each dye jar.

5. Set aside two beakers. Line up the rest of the beakers in front of the dye jars, one beaker directly in front of each dye jar. For each color, you will now have an empty beaker, a dye jar, and an empty labeled squirt bottle.

6. Fill the half-gallon container with 95° F (35° C) water.

7. Dip the measuring cup into the water, scoop out 1 cup, and pour it into the first beaker. Go down the line and put 1 cup of water into each beaker until you run out of beakers.

8. Put on your latex gloves, your dust mask or breathing apparatus, and safety goggles.

9. If you are using urea, measure 1 tablespoon into each beaker of water. Swirl each beaker to help the urea dissolve.

10. One by one, open each dye jar, take out 1 rounded tablespoon of dye powder, dump it into the matching beaker, and replace the jar lid. Remember to check suppliers' instructions,

as some colors require double the powder. Don't bother mixing the dye at this point. Put the jar back in front of its associated squirt bottle each time. Go to the next color on the right, and continue on down the line until you have run out of beakers. (Note: Since I'm not too concerned about contaminating the colors in the jar, I just rinse the mixing spoon when I'm done with the reds, the purples, and before the browns. If you'd rather, swirl the mixing spoon in the water and wipe it dry before going to the next jar.)

11 Make a "rinse" beaker by putting some clear water into one of the two extra beakers you had set aside.

12 Starting at the left, mix each beaker of dye using the stick mixer. After you mix the red, rinse the mixer by swirling it in the rinse beaker. Rinse after the purple, too.

13 You should have one extra beaker with a wide enough mouth to hold a squirt bottle. Use this extra beaker to catch spills as you pour the dye concentrate into the squirt bottle. To do this, put the first empty squirt bottle (labeled lemon yellow) into the extra beaker, remove the cap from the bottle, and put a funnel it. Hold onto the funnel as you pour the first beakerful of dye concentrate into the funnel. If the dye powder hasn't dissolved fully, pour the dye back into the "dirty" beaker, mix it some more, and pour it down the funnel into the squirt bottle again. When the dye is all in the bottle, put the cap back on the squirt bottle and close the cap. To test the cap seal, hold the squirt bottle over the "dirty" beaker, and gently turn it over; no dye should leak out.

14 Put the filled squirt bottle behind the dye jar. Keeping everything lined up is helpful to me; otherwise, I get confused and am not sure what color I've mixed.

15 Continue down the line, rinsing the funnel after the red, the purple, and before the browns.

Now you should have a lovely row of colored dye in bottles. At this point, you can clean up and go have lunch. Remember to keep your gloves on while you rinse out your tools, or you'll have multicolored hands! Once I've cleaned up, I throw all my mixing stuff into the half-gallon container so it's together the next time I need it.

Since we haven't added soda ash yet, the dyes are not reacting. The dye concentrates will store for several weeks if you keep them cool, meaning not in a hot garage. Refrigerating helps if you have a separate refrigerator—don't use the same one you keep food in.

THE PROCESS OF DYEING

To dye the fabric, we will start by soaking the fabric in very hot water that has been mixed with soda ash to reach a pH of 12. Then we will hang the fabric across a horizontal pole and pour the dye down the fabric. Before you begin, read through all of the steps.

1 To get the length of the fabric you will be able to dye, measure the height of the pole that you have hung over your drip catcher; subtract about 3", and then double this measurement. You don't want to suspend the fabric too high over the drip catcher because drips will splash out.

2 Rip or cut several pieces to the desired length. (I cut my fabric by clipping along the selvedge and ripping it.)

3 If you need to scour the fabric before you dye it, do that now.

4 Prepare your dye fixative (soda ash solution). Put 2–3 gallons of the hottest available tap water into the five-gallon bucket. If you have pH tape, pour about ½ cup of soda ash into the bucket and stir it. Then measure the pH and add more soda ash if necessary. If you don't have pH tape, add about 1 cup of soda ash to the bucket. Stir with the mixing stick.

When the soda ash has dissolved, throw in two pieces of fabric and push them beneath the water with the stick.

6 Let the fabric soak for about 5 minutes. I use this time to decide what colors I am going to dye.

7 Let's assume that for this piece, we will use fuchsia, red, orange, and yellow. Set those four squirt bottles near the dye space.

8 Wearing rubber gloves, pull one piece of fabric out of the soda ash soak, wring it out over the bucket, and hang it over the pole as if it's a sheet that's being line-dried. Line up the bottom edges of the fabric. Smooth the two layers together between your hands to get rid of air bubbles.

9 Push the two selvedges together towards each other along the top of the pole, as if you are gathering curtains. Slide your hands down the fabric to gently ring out excess water. Now pull on both selvedges, sideways, so that both layers stick together, and so that the fabric is spread out to about ⅔ of its original width. There should be lots of lovely vertical wrinkles in the fabric.

10 For your first color, take either the red or fuchsia dye bottle. You will make four stripes with this first color, randomly spaced across the width. Start at the top of the pole, about four inches in from one selvedge. Squeeze the bottle and a vertical line of dye will start down the fabric. Let the dye drip down by itself. The dye will stop about halfway down, so move the bottle down and continue to squirt out dye. Don't worry about making the line of dye go all the way to the bottom—⅔ of the way is fine. Do

check both layers of fabric to make sure the dye has soaked completely through. If necessary, squirt dye on both layers.

11 Apply the last two colors in the same way. Squirt dye right along the selvedge to make sure it's covered.

12 Now, look and see how much white fabric is still at the bottom of your fabric. You can either use more dye, or fill a squirt bottle with some liquid from the soda soak and pour it onto the fabric at the pole. This makes the color run down the fabric, giving more texture, but it also lightens the color a bit. You may find that the color is generally darker towards the top of the fabric than the bottom. I like this variation because it adds more breadth to my dyed fabric palette.

13 Check your fabric for other white areas. If you don't want them, squirt yellow onto the white. The yellow will blend in better than the fuchsia when doing "spot squirts." You can also dip a foam paintbrush into dye and paint a little bit onto the white spots.

14 If you have a long enough pole, slide this piece over to one side and dye a second fabric piece while the first one hangs. Try not to touch the first piece again or let the second piece rub up

Left: After a lighter shade of yellow and an orange have been added to the fabric using the pouring method, a foam brush can be dipped in dye to fill in white spaces, or a brush can be used to add small amounts of dye along the top of the fabric.

Right: Once all the desired colors have been put on, one way to make sure all the fabric has dye is to twist the fabric tightly.

DYEING DO'S AND DON'TS

- Don't go poking around at the dyed fabric while your gloves are dirty, or you'll get spots on it.

- If the soda soak water runs low, add more hot water and soda ash and recheck the pH with the pH tape.

- Empty the liquid in the drip catcher into a big bucket using a measuring cup, turkey baster, or bottle that you can squeeze to collect liquid. The idea is to leave the drip catcher on the floor while you empty it. Don't pick up the tray and carry it around.

- You may be delighted by the color of the dye that has collected in the drip catcher. Throw a piece of fabric in the dye soup in the catcher if you'd like. The color won't be that intense, but it will be mottled. If you don't like it that much, save that piece and do it again next time you dye. These pieces often end up making wonderful background fabrics.

against the first piece, especially if you are using different colors in the two pieces. If possible, leave the fabric on the pole to batch until it is dry or overnight, whichever comes first.

15 If you need the entire pole for the second piece, gently remove the first piece and lay it flat on a plastic-covered table if you have one, or twist it and put it in a plastic bag to batch.

16 The colors will be more intense the longer the fabric can stay wet and warm. In the summer, I sometimes wrap the pieces in plastic bags and let them batch on my driveway in the sun, or in the garage where it's like a sauna. I let my fabrics batch at least 24 hours to deepen the colors. If it's not convenient to wait that long, let them batch at least two hours. _(Note: It's OK to let the fabric batch for more than 24 hours if you forget to rinse it. But don't leave it so long it gets moldy, and consider that the soda ash could weaken the fibers over time if left wet too long.)_

RINSING

Once your fabric has batched in plastic for 2–24 hours, or it is dry (if you left it hung up on the pole), it's time to wash it and see what you have.

1 The first rinse is to remove soda ash and excess dye. Use cold water, as warm water won't help much. Cold water will also help keep the darker colors from staining the lighter sections. If my piece has blue and yellow, I rinse by hand in the laundry sink (don't use your bathtub). If the fabric is either all warm colors (yellow through reds) or cools (blue through greens), I throw it in the washing machine where I can rinse about 16 yards at a time.

2 The second rinse should be with hot water. Add some Synthrapol or Ivory dishwashing liquid to help release the excess dye and keep it from falling back onto the fabric.

3 For the final rinse, rinse in warm water until the water is clear. To check this, I dip a clear plastic glass into the water right after the machine starts agitating and hold the glass up to the light. (Be very careful to keep your body parts out of the machine during the spin cycle.) Holding it up gives you an idea of how many more rinse cycles you may need. Some colors rinse out faster than others. When rinsing long pieces, I pull the fabric out between cycles and straighten it out a little, so I don't have a washing machine full of dyed rope.

VARIATIONS

1. Use only one or two colors of dye, but vary the intensity of each color by diluting some of the dye concentrate in a separate squirt bottle.

2. Before you hang fabric on the pole to dye, dip the entire piece into a very diluted color to give a pale background color. Then hang up and dye.

3. After squirting dye onto the fabric, twist it tightly like a rope. Then let it batch.

4. Put some dye in a spray bottle and apply to the fabric while it is hanging up. Be careful not to get dye on other things in the area, like on your clean laundry.

5. Use a blended color and let the dye separate on the fabric into areas of its component colors. Test the dye first by putting a dot of dye on a scrap of fabric to see which blends will separate out.

Problem	Cause and solution
The yellow sections have splotches of other colors.	Color could have gotten onto the yellow either when you were dyeing the fabric, if you touched it with dirty rubber gloves, or if you let another piece touch it. It could also happen if a darker section rubbed up against the yellow during the first rinse cycle. ☑ Rinse by hand for the first round next time.
Fire spots	These spots come from lumps of dye. ☑ If they bother you, mix the dye concentrate better next time.
Not enough depth of color	The number one cause is incorrect fabric to start with. ☑ Increase the amount of dye powder, have longer batching, and make sure there is enough soda ash.
Some red dye concentrates "gel" when stored.	☑ Add urea at mixing. Or, just let the bottle sit in a warm water bath and the gel should melt.

Colorful combinations

Here are some color schemes you might want to try, using the colors I recommended for your initial purchase.

1. Both yellows, orange, scarlet, and fuchsia
2. Both yellows and just the orange
3. Orange, scarlet, and fuchsia
4. Scarlet, fuchsia, and turquoise
5. Fuchsia, turquoise, and the darker blue
6. Turquoise, the darker blue, and either one or both of the yellows
7. Fuchsia, grape, and either one or both of the blues
8. Both blues and grape
9. Mix up a green from the lighter yellow and turquoise, turquoise and grape.*
10. Yellow and both blues

*Remember that any time you mix all three primary colors together—red, blue, and yellow—you will get brown. If you mix complements together, you will get brown because all three colors are present (i.e., yellow and purple is actually mixing yellow, blue, and red). You can tone down a yellow by adding a bit of purple, and use that with the oranges and reds. If you put a purple stripe next to a yellow stripe, you will get brown where they mix. I have been able to put green, purple, and orange on one piece, being very careful and using a turkey baster to apply the color to try to avoid the colors mixing. Add dark colors sparingly.

If you buy a few blended colors, you can have even more fun. I recommend starting with the violets, and using them in the same piece as the pure grape, the blues, and the reds.

Right: "Guitar Trio" • 2005 • 17" x 23"

CHAPTER ONE:
BOISTEROUS BEGINNINGS

BLUE AND YELLOW DON'T MAKE GREEN
Michael Wilcox
Whitchurch, Bristol: Michael Wilcox School of
Color Publishing, LTD, 2002
ISBN: 0967962870

COLOR WORKS: THE CRAFTER'S GUIDE TO COLOR
Deb Menz
Loveland, CO: Interweave Press, 2004
ISBN: 1931499470

DESIGNER'S GUIDE TO COLOR 2
James Stockton
San Francisco, CA: Chronicle Books, 1984
ISBN: 0877013454

DESIGNER'S GUIDE TO COLOR 3
Jeanne Allen and Ikuyoshi Shibukawa
San Francisco, CA: Chronicle Books, 1986
ISBN: 0877014086

EXPLORING COLOR
Nita Leland
Cincinnati, OH: North Light Books, 1998
ISBN: 0891348468

PANTONE GUIDE TO COMMUNICATING WITH COLOR
Leatrice Eiseman
Sarasota, FL: Grafix Press, LTD, 2000
ISBN: 0966638328

CHAPTER THREE:
DESIGN YOUR OWN QUILT

CUBISM: COLOUR LIBRARY
(PHAIDON COLOUR LIBRARY)
COOPER PHILIP
London: Phaidon Press, 1995
ISBN: 0714832502

Left: Detail of "Watercolor Vases" • 2001 • 42" x 51"

DESIGN BASICS
David A. Lauer and Stephen Pentak
Fort Worth, TX: Harcourt College Publishers, 2000
ISBN: 0155083775

DESIGN MOTIFS OF ANCIENT MEXICO
Jorge Enciso
New York: Dover Publications, 1953
ISBN: 0486200841

DESIGNER'S GUIDE TO JAPANESE PATTERNS 2
Jeanne Allen
San Francisco, CA: Chronicle Books, 1988
ISBN: 0877015430

GEOMETRY OF DESIGN:
STUDIES IN PROPORTION AND COMPOSITION
Kimberly Elam
New York: Princeton Architectural Press, 2001
ISBN: 1568982496

NOTAN: THE DARK-LIGHT PRINCIPLE OF DESIGN
Dorr Bothwell and Marlys Mayfield
New York: Dover Publications, 1991
ISBN: 048626856X

THE COMPLETE GUIDE TO CREATIVE WATERCOLOR
Miles G. Batt
Fort Lauderdale, FL: Creative Art Publications, 1988
ISBN: 096193865X

CHAPTER FOUR: FREE-MOTION QUILTING

ART DECO ORNAMENTAL IRONWORK
Henri Martinie
New York: Dover Publications, 1995
ISBN: 0486285359

GUIDE TO MACHINE QUILTING
Diane Gaudynski
Paducah, KY: American Quilter's Society, 2002
ISBN: 1574327968

HANDBOOK OF ORNAMENT
Franz Sales Meyer
New York: Dover Publications, 1957
ISBN: 0486203026

JAPANESE DESIGN MOTIFS: 4260 ILLUSTRATIONS OF HERALDIC CRESTS.
Compiled by the Matsuya Piece-Goods Store.
Translated, with a new intro by Fumie Adachi.
New York: Dover Publications, 1972
ISBN: 0486228746

JAPANESE BORDER DESIGNS
Selected and edited by Theodore Menten
New York: Dover Publications, 1975
ISBN: 0486231801

APPENDIX B: DYEING TO GET STARTED

COLOR BY ACCIDENT: LOW-WATER IMMERSION DYEING
Ann Johnston
Lake Oswego, OR: Ann Johnston, 1997
ISBN: 0965677605

COLOR BY DESIGN: PAINT AND PRINT WITH DYE
Ann Johnston
Lake Oswego, OR: Ann Johnston, 2001
ISBN: 0965677613

COMPLEX CLOTH: A COMPREHENSIVE GUIDE TO SURFACE DESIGN
Jane Dunnewold
Bothell, WA: Fiber Studio Press, 1996
ISBN: 1564771490

DYES & PAINTS: A HANDS-ON GUIDE TO COLORING FABRIC
Elin Noble
Bothell, WA: Fiber Studio Press, 1998
ISBN: 1564771032

MICKEY LAWLER'S SKYDYES:
A VISUAL GUIDE TO FABRIC PAINTING.
Mickey Lawler
Lafayette, CA: C&T Pub, 1999
ISBN: 157120072X

Free Expression: The Art and Confessions of a Contemporary Quilter

Left: "Queen of Cups" • 2000 • 66" x 81"

About the author

Robbi Joy Eklow and Brian, her husband of 25 years, graduated from the Purdue University School of Engineering in Indiana in 1980, and have lived in and around Chicago ever since. Their two children, Joshua and Samantha, are students at the University of Iowa. They are majoring in liberal arts because they think engineering is boring.

Robbi started sewing at a young age, while watching moon launches. Her first project was a shirt she made by tracing the pattern off a jumper. She sewed it together with no facings or hems—just two pieces of fabric, and by hand because her mother was sure she'd sew through her finger if let anywhere near a sewing machine. Her mother did let her wear her shirt in public, however, and that encouraged Robbi to keep going.

Robbi started her first quilt in 1976, during the Great Quilt Revival. It was a Drunkard's Path in red, white, and blue, cut out with an electric scissors. The pieces didn't fit together very well and the blocks disappeared into the dorm storage facility, never to be seen again. She started quilting again in 1981 during an extremely cold winter. She'd forage for fabric and then stay home and play with it. But she never finished anything until right before son Josh was born, when she finally took up quilting in earnest. She has been quilting ever since.

Robbi has written a first-person humor column on her adventures in quilting, *Goddess of the Last Minute*, for Quilting Arts Magazine®, since Summer 2002. She teaches nationally and her work has been exhibited in major shows where she occasionally wins a ribbon.

To date, she has not sewn through her finger.